The 10
STUPIDEST MISTAKES
MEN MAKE
WHEN FACING DIVORCE

The 10
STUPIDEST MISTAKES
MEN MAKE
WHEN FACING DIVORCE

AND HOW TO AVOID THEM

Joseph Cordell, Esq.

THREE RIVERS PRESS

NEW YORK

Published in the United States by Three Rivers Press,
an imprint of the Crown Publishing Group,
a division of Random House, Inc., New York.
www.threeriverspress.com

Three Rivers Press and the Tugboat design
are registered trademarks of Random House, Inc.

Library of Congress Cataloging-in-Publication Data

Cordell, Joseph E.
The 10 stupidest mistakes men make when facing divorce and how to avoid
them / by Joseph Cordell.—1st ed.
  1. Divorce—Law and legislation—United States—Popular
works. I. Title. II. Title: Ten stupidest mistakes men make when facing
divorce and how to avoid them.
KF535.Z9C67 2010
346.7301'66—dc22   2010002423

ISBN 978-0-307-58980-4

Printed in the United States of America

Design by Cindy LaBreacht

ACKNOWLEDGMENTS

M Y NAME IS ON the cover of this book, just as my name is on the building at our law firm's headquarters in St. Louis, and on the doors of our branch offices across the country. But this book, like the firm in a much larger sense, would not have been possible without the help of many people. Indeed, I should start these acknowledgments by thanking all the lawyers who have worked with me over the years. I've learned something from every one of them, and we continue to share information and strategy, and to learn from each other in order to better represent men in domestic relations cases.

I need to thank several of our lawyers particularly, for taking their personal time to contribute so many comments, observations, and case studies that enrich this book with their up-to-the-minute insights on this ever-evolving area of law, and for their many real-life examples and experiences. Foremost among the contributors was Scott Trout, the managing partner of our firm, who is one of the most highly respected attorneys in the field and also one of my most trusted advisors and closest friends for many years.

Besides offering invaluable insights from his experiences in and out of court, Richard Coffee was essential in helping refine and shape the manuscript. In working with Richard on this project, it became clear to me that he could have written his own book about divorce for men—but I am extremely grateful that he helped with mine instead. Other lawyers in our far-flung offices who contributed to this book include Allison Cunningham, also a partner in the firm, along with Dorothy Ripka, Spencer Williams, Jill Best, Frank Murphy, Kristen Zurek, Connie Cho,

Lisa Adams, Andy Ordyna, and Andy VanNess. From our corporate staff, Keri Esmar, Rick Ortiz, and Paul McMahon used their sharp eyes and their finely honed way with words to help in the editing and proofreading of the manuscript.

I also owe my thanks to Timothy Harper, the journalist-lawyer-professor who helped so much with the organizing and writing of this book. I'd heartily recommend Tim, who is based at www.timharper.com, to any aspiring author who needs help negotiating the convoluted shoals of publishing in the twenty-first century. Our agent, Nancy Love, showed great confidence in this project from the first time we mentioned it to her. Her considerable abilities are the reason this book found a home at Crown Publishers, where our editor, Nathan Roberson, showed a deft hand and offered insightful encouragement. It's clear why so many people in the book world believe Nathan is going to be a force in the publishing industry for many years to come.

As always, in this and every other meaningful endeavor in my life, none of it would have been possible without the love and support of my family: my wife Yvonne, who founded Cordell & Cordell with me nearly two decades ago, and our beautiful daughters Elizabeth and Caroline.

Finally, this book would never have been possible without the generosity, spirit, and compassion of the men that I—and the lawyers in my firm—have represented across the country and across the years. The selfless commitment of these men to what is right and what is fair—not so much for themselves, but for their children—is the real inspiration for our work, and for this book. Thank you, men. Keep fighting for your rights, and for your children.

Joseph Cordell
St. Louis, Missouri

CONTENTS

Introduction 1

Stupid Mistake No. 1
MOVING OUT 7

Stupid Mistake No. 2
CHOOSING THE WRONG LAWYER 29

Stupid Mistake No. 3
WAITING FOR YOUR WIFE TO FILE 54

Stupid Mistake No. 4
CONCEALING INFORMATION FROM YOUR LAWYER 80

Stupid Mistake No. 5
NEGLECTING THE CHILDREN 105

Stupid Mistake No. 6
DOING A SLOPPY JOB ON FINANCIAL RECORDS 125

Stupid Mistake No. 7
TALKING TOO MUCH—ESPECIALLY TO YOUR WIFE 148

Stupid Mistake No. 8
REVEALING TOO MUCH ON THE INTERNET 166

Stupid Mistake No. 9
FAILING TO FULLY ENGAGE IN YOUR CASE 179

Stupid Mistake No. 10
BEING ILL-PREPARED FOR TESTIMONY AND INTERVIEWS 194

Looking Ahead 221

Index 223

The 10 STUPIDEST MISTAKES MEN MAKE WHEN FACING DIVORCE

DIVORCE IS ONE of the most daunting things a man can face in life. It's like trying to walk across a vast swampland—but with heavy boots on your feet and a blindfold over your eyes. You never know when you're going to step into quicksand, and it's easy to find yourself in over your head before you know it. It's easy to make mistakes. Most men do.

You don't have to be stupid to make a stupid mistake during a divorce, and you definitely don't have to be a bad husband or father. Smart, fair-minded, hardworking, good men make all sorts of mistakes in divorce. Executives and professors and doctors make the same mistakes that plumbers and truck drivers make. Indeed, sometimes the professional men make *more* mistakes.

What's crazy is that many of these stupid mistakes happen when men are trying to do the right thing. They don't know how to negotiate their way through the legal and judicial processes, their good intentions backfire, and before they know it they have dug their own graves. Much of the time, the worst mistakes don't even seem like mistakes until later, when men suddenly realize that those seemingly innocuous or well-intentioned actions in fact had disastrous, life-changing consequences. When a divorce goes badly for a man—financially, or in terms of seeing his children—it's usually because of one of the 10 Stupidest Mistakes in this book.

This book is for any man facing divorce—including you. Maybe you are looking forward to being divorced. Maybe you're the one who's pulling the plug on the marriage. Or maybe it wasn't your decision. Maybe you're angry. And hurt. Maybe you're worried because she's threatening to take the children and keep you from seeing them. Maybe you don't have kids, or your kids are grown, and your biggest concern is that you don't want to get screwed financially. No matter who you are, the Stupid Mistakes are lurking out there in that swamp called divorce, waiting for you to make a misstep. This book can help you kick off the heavy boots and pull away the blindfold as you walk through the swamp, and can help you recognize the quicksand and the sinkholes. This is your map to high ground and safety.

The 10 Stupidest Mistakes: This book will tell you exactly what they are, and then exactly how to avoid them—and the many other smaller mistakes that grow out of them. This is the first book on divorce—the one book on divorce—that gives thoughtful men all the basic information and strategies they need in divorce. The book, of course, is not merely about how to avoid a handful of common mistakes. It's about the tactics—and the attitudes—that men can embrace to get through divorce and emerge healthier and happier than ever. No matter what your goals—protecting your relationship with your kids, holding on to your property, minimizing your monthly payments, or all of the above—the goal of this book is for you to come out of your divorce in one piece, with the lifestyle you'd like and the freedom to build a new, full, and happy life.

The book is organized in a roughly chronological sequence, starting with the most common mistakes men make early in the divorce process. Every divorce is different, of course. There's no cookie-cutter, one-size-fits-all formula. But this book proceeds through the major mistakes many men make, in the order in which they often occur. We hope that not all the mistakes apply to you and your case. But all or most of them might. By reading this book and following the advice, you'll know how to avoid the 10 Stupidest Mistakes, and how to deal with them if you've already made a mistake.

How do I, Joe Cordell, know what the mistakes are? How do I know how to avoid them? How do I know what advice to offer for overcoming a mistake you've already made? There's a simple, powerful answer: experience. My colleagues and I have been there. We've walked the walk, step by step, alongside tens of thousands of men. We continue to handle thousands of new cases every year. You can't make a mistake we haven't seen, and overcome.

This book is based on real men in real cases. I tell their stories, though I've changed the names and some of the details for privacy reasons. Look through some of the cases, some of the stories of the real men in these pages. The men's stories, the legal analysis, and the strategic advice presented in this book are the result of decades of practice, thousands of cases, and the combined experiences of many of the most seasoned men's divorce lawyers in the nation.

Start with Mistake No. 1, or just open the book anywhere. You'll see similarities to your case—and dangers you can avoid. You may see weaknesses in your preconceptions, and how what seems like doing the right thing today isn't always the right thing in the long term.

As you think about divorce, it might seem like your wife has an unfair advantage—and it's entirely possible that she does. The judicial system—lawyers, judges, social workers, and the court administration—is prone to assume without proof that:

✗ Moms should be the primary custodial parents;
✗ Men accused of abuse must be guilty;
✗ Men alleging abuse are lying or overreacting;

✗ Women are not as capable of generating income as men;

✗ Men are less deserving of assets earned by a woman than the reverse.

My career as a lawyer, my firm, and now this book are devoted to fighting those and other assumptions that are unfair to men. The goal of this book is to undercut those assumptions and take away her advantages. Believe it or not, it is possible to level the playing field—you just have to know how.

Our firm, Cordell & Cordell, P.C., was founded in 1990 as a general practice firm focusing on domestic relations matters. With offices in two dozen cities across America, we have evolved into one of the nation's largest domestic relations firms for men, who now make up 98 percent of our clientele. But you don't have to hire me or one of my attorneys to represent you in your divorce. Take this book to your own lawyer and use it to help develop the strategy and tactics for your case. The odds are that your lawyer will have heard of us. Your lawyer may even be among the thousands of attorneys who have come to us—our conferences, seminars, panel discussions, and online resources—for information and training on how to represent men in divorce. When lawyers at other firms need to bone up on the latest developments in divorce, or when they have particularly troublesome cases, Joe Cordell and his firm are where they go for information and help. To put it bluntly, there is simply no more authoritative source on divorce for men in America. This book is a summary of the main points we think all men need to know from the very first moments they realize that their marriages may be in trouble. This book, like our firm, aims to give men hope, and to empower them. We want to assure men that they and their lawyers can aggressively pursue their interests and the interests of their children despite the common stereotypes and biases within the legal system.

Finally, this book is written by a man for other men. It's written in the way we talk and think. The legal principles are sound, but they are explained without the legal mumbo jumbo. It moves fast. It's an easy read. And every single lesson in here is one that you need to know.

MOVING OUT

BILL WAS A successful architect, with his own small firm. He was married to Ellen, his college sweetheart, and they had two daughters, ages six and eight. They enjoyed a comfortable upper-middle-class lifestyle—a nice home, a couple of late-model cars, one or two vacations a year. Bill loved family life. Even if he had to stay late at work, he almost always made it home to read the girls their bedtime stories. In the mornings, he got them both up, made sure they were dressed and had their homework, prepared their breakfast, helped them pack their lunches, and then drove them to school on his way in to the office. Ellen was not a morning person, but that was okay with Bill. He liked having the morning as his special time with the girls.

The marriage was good, he thought, but not great. Lately Ellen was spending more and more time out during the day, playing tennis and shopping and having lunch with her friends. She had begun asking her mom to pick up the girls after school sometimes. Bill didn't always know where his wife was or what she was doing, but he didn't want to press her. Being a stay-at-home mom was tough, he reasoned. And besides, the girls loved going to Grandma's house.

One Sunday evening after he tucked the girls in, Bill

came downstairs to find Ellen waiting for him at the kitchen table.

"Sit down," she said. "We need to talk."

She wanted a divorce. He was stunned. "Why?" he stammered. "What's wrong?"

"I'm just not happy," she said. "I don't love you anymore."

Bill couldn't believe it. He didn't want his marriage to end. He wanted to try to work things out. This was so sudden. He pleaded with her to be patient, to keep trying. He'd change. He'd do whatever she wanted. He pressed her: What else could he do?

"Nothing," she said. "You just don't make me happy." That was all she could tell him, and she kept saying it over and over: "You just don't make me happy."

Ellen wanted Bill to move out that night. He could go stay with his parents, who lived a few miles away.

"No," he said.

"If you don't," she said, "I will call the police. I'll tell them you hit me. They'll take you away in handcuffs. And I'll get a restraining order that keeps you out of the house anyway. I'll keep you away from the kids, too. Do you want to see the kids? Then move out now."

Reeling, Bill felt like he had no choice. What could he do at ten o'clock on a Sunday night? If he was arrested, even on a false charge, he couldn't imagine the damage to his reputation. He'd probably lose his business.

"I want a divorce, but I want it to be civilized," Ellen assured him. "If you move out tonight, I'll let you see the girls as much as you want until we get everything settled. I don't want to hurt you. I just want out of the marriage."

Bill threw a few things into an overnight bag and drove to his parents' house. That drive was the longest 15 minutes of his life.

The next morning, Bill called my law firm and asked if he could come in. An hour later he was sitting in my office. I've seen a lot of unhappy men sit in that chair across from me. Sometimes they are angry. Sometimes they are sad. Sometimes they are frustrated. Sometimes they feel like they have failed as husbands. Sometimes they just don't understand what is happening. Bill was all of those.

"I don't know what to do," he said. "What should I do?"

I explained to Bill, as gently but as firmly as I could, that he had already made a big mistake. I also told him—though it didn't make him feel much better—that he wasn't alone. Moving out is the first mistake many men make when their marriages are on the rocks. And, unfortunately, it's often the biggest mistake, too—the one that has the biggest impact as they try to rebuild their lives after the divorce. Moving out when it's not necessary can mean that a man gets to see his kids less and that the divorce costs more than if he stayed in the family home as long as reasonably possible.

Many men voluntarily—though reluctantly—move out because they think it is the right thing to do. Maybe it will help save the marriage. Maybe it will make things easier on his wife and kids during a difficult time. I think some men see the family home as a place where they can live as long as their wives agree. For whatever reason, men want to do the presumed right thing—even when their marriages are collapsing and the world is crashing down around them. Besides, if the marriage is struggling and there are tensions in the home, it often makes sense to take a break. A little time apart might ease the tension, especially if there are children at home. And who knows? Maybe a temporary separation ultimately will lead to a reconciliation and help save the marriage.

Those are noble sentiments, but foolish. Many men think they have to move out when the relationship falls apart, but in most cases they don't—and they shouldn't.

My lawyers have witnessed this scene many times: A man comes in for the first time and says, "My wife just told me she wants a divorce. So I went to stay with a friend. Now I'm looking for an apartment."

We ask why. Why did he move out? The man seems confused. "She said she wants a divorce," he says. "The marriage is over. We're not a couple anymore. We're not going to live together."

But why, we ask, do you assume you are the one who should move out?

"Uh, I thought I was supposed to," he says. He explains that she doesn't want him around the house anymore, and it felt like he should leave. He didn't want to fight with her, especially in front of the kids. It made him uncomfortable to be there—to be anywhere he wasn't wanted anymore.

It's amazing to us how many times the man will voluntarily move out even when the wife is in the wrong. A common example is when the wife is cheating, announces to her husband that her future is with her new man, demands a divorce, and tells him to get out. And many men do it.

"No," we tell them. "Don't do it. Don't leave. She's the one who wants the marriage to end. If someone has to leave, she should be the one, not you. If she wants her space, she can pack up her things and leave."

Many men who come to us are discouraged when we tell them they shouldn't have moved out—they've already made Stupid Mistake No. 1. But for many of those men, it's a mistake that can be undone. If there haven't been any legal proceedings

Move back in

dictating he has to leave, it's one of those rare instances when the man gets a do-over. For you golfers, a mulligan.

> *Move back in. Right now. As soon as possible. The less time you have been gone, the better.*

We tell men who have moved out: "Nothing has been filed yet. Move back in. Right now. As soon as possible. The less time you have been gone, the better." The less time you're away, the less opportunity she has to claim you don't care about the kids or the house.

IF YOU MUST GO . . .

Of course, sometimes there are legitimate reasons for moving out, especially if the soon-to-be-ex-wife is making it impossible to stay. Unfortunately, if the police are called or the wife seeks an emergency protective order, the presumption remains that the wife will not make false accusations and the man is in the better financial and physical position to leave. If the police are called or a judge is given only the wife's version of the situation, it is more than likely the man will be told to leave. All your wife has to assert is aggressive conduct—blocking her path, taking her cell phone, verbal threats—and police or court intervention is probable. The bottom-line caveat: If you think there's any chance of a claim of violence or interference—by anyone, for any reason—then moving out may be necessary, at least for a few days until things calm down.

It's understandable that a man would want to avoid conflict and protect his kids from seeing their parents fighting. Those are admirable reasons for leaving. But it sends the wrong message, and what seems like a short-term solution to avoid conflict and make the breakup go smoothly can actually result in long-range problems and give the man a very rough ride when it comes to the details of the divorce. Instead of leaving, propose reasonable rules to continue cohabiting with minimum conflict. If she is adamant, propose a timetable that allows for an orderly evaluation of any transition. And always get to a lawyer immediately, preferably before you pack that bag.

There are a number of reasons that men should not move out. Most important is that staying in the family home allows the father to stay fully involved with his children during the divorce proceedings. We hear it all the time. In one breath, dads tell us, "I've moved out." In the next breath they say, "I want custody of my kids." At that point we have to advise our clients that having moved out, they may have limited the available strategies and increased the necessary effort and expense in pursuing custody. The divorce process can take time, especially when custody is an issue. If the father has moved out he may be portrayed as the "absentee father" or as having "moved on" without his children.

Here's how it works. Divorce proceedings are finalized one of two ways. One, the two parties can reach an out-of-court settlement and agree on custody and the division of property. Their lawyers take this settlement to the court, and the court reviews it. Unless there is something totally out of whack—something so unfair that it's clear at least one side's lawyer did a poor job—the court will approve the settlement and it will become official. The divorce decree will be entered and the two sides will be legally obliged to live up to their commitments.

But when the two sides cannot reach an out-of-court agreement to settle their divorce, it goes to court. There is a trial before a judge (a couple of states allow jury trials in some divorce cases, but it is rare) with witnesses and evidence and testimony and opening and closing arguments and rulings from the bench and, finally, a decision by the judge. That decision is the divorce decree, and the two sides are legally obliged to live up to its terms.

But none of that happens quickly. It may take months, or even a year or two, for a divorce case to get to trial. Even if both sides are eager to settle their divorce out of court, there are bound to be delays with lawyers and court schedules, and that can take weeks or months too.

In custody contests, the continued daily interaction with your children and intimate awareness of the details of their day is key. Moving out often means the father is cut off from the details of what is going on with his children, either by default or by the wife's design. Being out of the home allows the wife the opportunity to lobby, bribe, or guilt-trip the children in an attempt to alienate them from you. Let me put this very clearly: If you move out, you're setting up arguments and tactics used to deny you a reasonable chance of becoming the parent with primary custody.

> *In custody contests, the continued daily interaction with your children and intimate awareness of the details of their day is key.*

Agreeing to the wife's demand that you move out may also weaken any hope for meaningful joint custody. It is not uncommon for the wife who has gotten the husband to leave quickly to then propose a quick custody agreement. Ellen did that in the earlier example, claiming, "If you move out tonight, I'll let you see the girls as much as you want until we get everything settled." Believing that she has established that she is in control of the terms of the divorce by getting you to leave, she may propose a joint-custody agreement that contains a catchall provision. In the event of disagreement, her parenting decision prevails. Or she may agree to joint custody with no real expectation of having to abide by it. She assumes the man will automatically agree to whatever decisions she makes, regardless of his rights under the terms of joint custody.

So what happens during those weeks or months—or year or more—while the divorce is pending if you do voluntarily move out? Who decides who pays for what and who is responsible for the kids on what days?

Many states issue temporary orders to decide all that. These orders are often issued or approved by a judge after an initial hearing that is held soon after the divorce has been filed. The husband and wife, through their lawyers, usually work out the details between them. If they differ—on how much money the husband needs to pay the wife each week or month, for example, or how often he is allowed to take the kids overnight—their lawyers present their respective arguments and the court makes the ultimate decision. Either side can ask for another hearing to change the temporary orders, but in most cases, unless there is a severe problem with the temporary orders, the orders stand until the divorce is finalized. Judges don't want to hear the same temporary issues over and over.

Consequently, temporary orders are huge. Don't let anyone—especially your own lawyer—tell you otherwise. Let's use an example to illustrate. Alex and Zoe had not been getting along for years, and agreed to split up. They agreed to be civilized. He would move out and get an apartment near the family house, where she would continue to live with the kids, ages 11 and 14. The kids would stay with her during the week, in order not to interrupt their school routines. Alex could see the kids, both boys, any time he wanted after school. Both of them were athletes, and he could always go watch their games or practices and walk them home afterward. Alex could also see the kids on weekends, and he often did. He'd spend part of pretty much every Saturday or

Sunday with one or both. Because his apartment was too small to have both boys stay overnight at the same time, the kids stayed with him on alternate weekends. One would sleep at his place on Friday and Saturday, and then the other would stay with him the following Friday and Saturday.

These arrangements went on for some time as Alex and Zoe discussed the divorce and retained attorneys. The arrangement was approved by the court for the temporary orders issued shortly after Zoe finally filed for divorce. Alex was fine with the arrangements. For all practical purposes, Alex believed he had joint custody. He was in the process of getting a bigger place in the neighborhood, a place where each boy could have his own room, and he wanted 50-50 custody. But when he tried to formalize the 50-50 arrangement in the final divorce decree months later, he got a rude shock. Zoe said no. She wanted primary custody. She would allow Alex to have one or both boys one night each week and on alternate weekends.

In court, Alex's lawyer objected to Zoe's proposal. The judge seemed sympathetic to Alex's case: He was a good dad, he was involved. But the judge had a problem. If Alex had wanted 50-50 custody, why hadn't he asked for it earlier? Why hadn't he asked for it when he and Zoe were making the arrangements to split up almost a year ago?

Alex's lawyer tried to argue that Alex had agreed to the temporary orders solely because he thought that arrangement would be easiest for the kids during a difficult time.

Zoe's lawyer had a counterpoint. The arrangement had been working for a year. The kids were fine. Why change it now? Nothing was different except that their parents were not going to be officially married anymore. They were doing fine living with Mom and seeing Dad a few times a week. If Alex thought that arrangement was best for the kids up to that point and agreed to formalize the arrangement in the temporary order, why wasn't it still the best arrangement for them now?

Here's how one of our lawyers explains it to clients:

"Temporary orders are a significant strategy portion of the case. The judge will order who's living in the house and who's going to leave the house. Usually the primary parent will end up staying in the house with the children. If the dad moves out of the house by agreement without making a case before the judge as to primary responsibility for the kids, then that dad has a very hard case to make later to be the primary parent. Voluntarily leaving the house shows the court that clearly the dad doesn't even think that he is as crucial to this home as the mom is. Caseworkers tell me this all the time: If the dad believes that he is such a crucial part of the family that he'd be a good primary parent, well, he'd make the effort to stay in the home with the children if at all possible."

Staying in the home also makes sense for financial considerations, such as the additional cost of setting up a separate household for the husband and making sure two sets of household bills get paid. If the husband is directly paying the bills to support the household where they are both living, the wife needs less money, if any, from him, particularly if she has her own income to cover her personal expenses. Conversely, if the husband is out of the house, her attorney will seek to have him pay her temporary support so she can pay the household expenses, with no guarantee that she will actually use those payments for those bills. While the wife should be held accountable if she doesn't pay the household bills, the creditors don't care why the bills weren't paid and your credit takes a beating. Staying in

Staying in the home also makes sense for financial considerations.

the house and paying the expenses directly is less expensive and minimizes the debts that will have to be resolved in the final hearing.

Remember, the wife has no automatic priority to stay in the house, especially if she says she can't afford the mortgage payments on her own. When she asserts that you should make all or part of the monthly payments to let her stay in the home, you want to assert your right to comparable housing for you and your children. You shouldn't have to pay for her to have a better lifestyle than you do, especially if keeping her in high style means you can't pay your bills. Here's a common argument our lawyers make: "Your Honor, she cannot make the mortgage payments, but has family to stay with nearby. Our client can pay the mortgage, but doesn't have any family nearby. Since my client is going to have to pay the mortgage, then he should be allowed to stay in the house." That argument can be powerfully persuasive to some judges, simply because it's fair. If you're paying for the roof, you should be able to sleep under it.

In the case of a hostile divorce, being out of the house can open the door to what lawyers call "spousal mischief." One client who was not represented by our firm when he moved out came to us later with a sad story. He had initially agreed to pay the mortgage while his wife stayed in the house.

"But you gotta pay the utilities," he told her.

"No," she said. "You should pay the utilities, too."

"If you don't pay the utilities, I won't pay the mortgage," he insisted.

Finally they compromised on a temporary agreement approved by the court: She would pay for gas and electric, and he would pay the water bill. They agreed that she would pay all the bills as they came in during the divorce proceedings, and he would reimburse her for the water bill when the divorce be-came final. Well, it took a year for them to settle the details of the divorce. When he finally got the water bill, he learned that she had turned on the water taps in the house and left them run-ning 24/7 for every hour, every minute, every second of those 12 months. Neither he nor his previous lawyer had put any sort of contingency into the temporary agreement to limit the use of water or the amount of the bill. Consequently, he had to pay that huge water bill.

Damage to the house can be an issue, too. If you're in the house, you're going to be taking care of the place, as usual. If not, things can get run-down pretty fast. Often in a divorce one side or the other will try to hold on to the house. Sometimes it works, sometimes it doesn't. Sometimes the house has to be put on the market quickly, and sold quickly, for whatever price. In a few months, a house that has been neglected can lose a lot of value—and you can lose a lot of the equity that you had built up. That's usually money you were hoping to use to restart your life.

In one case I had, the husband moved out reluctantly and the wife stayed in the house to keep raising the kids there. But she couldn't afford the mortgage and let the payments slide without telling him. Before long the house was in foreclosure. She walked away and left the keys for the bank. In another case, the wife who stayed in the house let it fall into disrepair, and all the money and work my client had put into the place literally crumbled. In both cases, my clients didn't know what was going on, and by the time they learned about it, it was too late to do anything. Beyond the loss of the value of the house, they were co-debtors on the mort-gages so their credit ratings were trashed too.

In practical terms, moving out also means the husband is abandoning any hope of keeping the house to live in himself someday. I vividly remember asking a judge to award the house to a man who had moved out.

"What?" the judge demanded, looking at me as if I was crazy. "If he wanted the house, why did he move out?"

The man did not get the house.

One of the biggest problems with moving out is what you leave behind. Take a <u>detailed inventory</u> of what's in the house, down to the knives and forks, and document it with photos and videos if possible. Your lawyer will want to itemize the property left with your wife—and the longer and more valuable the list, the better for you when negotiating a financial settlement. For example, your soon-to-be-ex-wife might go to court saying that she needs money from you to buy new furniture or dishes or something else for the house. If you have an inventory, with photos, showing that you left behind a well-stocked house of good-quality furnishings, she won't get far with those arguments.

Lots of men leave behind their financial and personal documents, thinking they can retrieve them when needed. Whether they're joint documents showing accounts and tax returns, or your personal health, employment, or military records, take them with you.

"We're going to need to go through your financial records," I tell every client.

Far too many of them say, "Uh, I left 'em at the house." When they go back to retrieve the documents, the documents have disappeared.

When that happens, the man's attorney is in the awkward position of having to request all the financial information from the wife's attorney.

More than once we've gotten the response, "We don't know what you're talking about. We can't find any records like that."

I'll tell the other lawyer, "My client says the bank statements are in the basement in the southeast corner in the second drawer of the filing cabinet."

The wife's lawyer will come back a few days later and say, "My client says there are no documents."

We can re-create those records by going back to the financial institutions, but it can take a lot of time and add to the cost of the case.

Another consideration when moving out is your stuff. You know what I mean. All men have their stuff. Some of it may be valuable, some of it may be sentimental, and some of it may be meaningless to anyone but us. But it's our stuff and it's irreplaceable. It's also property your wife will use to gain leverage or will dispose of in an attempt to trigger an angry reaction to hold against you later.

If and when you do move out, make sure you take your most important personal property with you. You may think you'll always be able to get your prize shotguns or your baseball card collection, but when you walk out that door it may be the last time you see them. In the heat of the moment, amid all the emotion, men throw a few things in a bag and they're gone. Later, when they return, their stuff is gone too. Sure, when men leave, their wives promise to let them come back and get their stuff. But sometimes they don't let them in again. Sometimes they just throw the stuff away or, worse yet, give it to their new boyfriends.

When anticipating the wife's request for you to leave or when negotiating the possible timetable for any voluntary departure, build in time to move your things. Rent storage space or use a friend's garage, and move what you can. I am not talking about taking the furniture or appliances, which will certainly trigger alarms with your wife and perhaps escalate matters (although more than one client's wife has backed up a truck while he was at work and cleaned out the house, including appliances and kitchen cabinets). Moving out your tools, sporting equipment, and records that your wife never sees or uses should not cause her concern. If she objects to you moving your stuff, that's a red flag: This divorce may not be amicable after all.

> *If she objects to you moving your stuff, that's a red flag: This divorce might not be amicable after all.*

Sometimes it's too late to go back, such as when the wife has formally filed for divorce and the papers have been served on the husband. In some states, that means the case has been "frozen" and all the people and property have to remain in place until the case is settled. Once papers have been served, the husband may have to go to court and ask a judge to order the wife to let him back in.

When men have moved out and want to move back, we advise against barging in like the king of the castle. That might inflame the wife, create a scene, and upset the kids. We tell them to move back in with little fanfare, preferably when no one else is home. Avoiding the drama is always a big part of managing a breakup. You want to avoid any situation that might produce harsh words, shouting, and especially violence. "Don't disturb the peace when you move back in," we tell clients.

But that phrase—disturbing the peace—has different meanings in different communities. One client who lived in a small town and knew some of the local police went to talk to them before he moved back in, just to find out what he could do if his wife had changed the locks or blocked the doors. "Hey, it's your house," the officer told him. "We don't care how you get in. You're entitled to break a window to get into your own house." As long as your name is on the deed or lease, you generally have the right to enter your home, as long as you don't create a disturbance. Just to be safe, check with your attorney or local law enforcement before reentering your home.

On more than one occasion, a man has asked me, "Well, where should I sleep? Should I move to the basement? Out to the garage?"

"What are the options, what are the schedules, and what makes sense?" I ask them. "If you want to stay in the master bedroom to get a good night's sleep since you have to go to work and she doesn't, stake that claim. You've got as much right to stay there as your wife. If she doesn't want to sleep in the same room, she can go out on the couch or to a guest room."

At the same time, sure, if a man says he'd be more comfortable in a guest room or on a foldout in the basement, by all means that's where he should sleep—especially if it will hold down tension in the home. Even if the judge kicks the husband out as part of the temporary orders after a contested hearing, that's okay. That's better than leaving voluntarily. By asserting reasonable arguments to stay in *your* house with *your* children you have a stronger position when it comes to asking for custody or the house in the final divorce settlement.

GETTING BACK IN

When Bill, the architect in the example at the beginning of this chapter, moved out of the house, he came to me and asked, "What should I do?" He still hoped to save his marriage. "I don't think it's necessarily over," he kept saying.

We told him that we admired his commitment to his family and his desire to hold the marriage together, but we also told him he was probably being naïve. When things get as far as

naïve

this—being <u>forced out of</u> the house under the threat of arrest when he hadn't laid a finger on his wife—we rarely see couples reconcile.

When we learned that Bill's wife had not yet served him with divorce papers, <u>I urged him to move back in.</u> "Resume your normal role. Read to the kids. Make them breakfast. Drive them to school."

We advised him to go back that very afternoon, while his wife was picking up the kids from school. "Just be there when she gets home," I suggested.

Bill was uncomfortable with the idea. He had always gone out of his way to be accommodating to Ellen and her wishes and needs. It was against his nature to do anything that might upset her, and he was sure she would be very upset to find him back in the house. But after a 20-minute discussion, part pep talk about how it might actually help his marriage and part point-by-point legal argument on the advantages of staying in the home for both financial and custody reasons, he agreed to move back in.

He called me a few hours later, around the time school was getting out.

"<u>I can't get back in,</u>" he said. "<u>She's already changed the locks.</u>" She must have made the appointment with the locksmith before she asked him to move out.

I said he could still move back in. I urged him to call the local police—it was a nice suburb, the police knew this sort of thing happened, and they knew how to handle it—and see what they said. Maybe they would help him get back in, the way they might help any homeowner who accidentally locked himself out of his house.

"Okay, let me think about that," Bill said. He didn't call back until the next day, when he reported that he had given up on getting back into the house. He didn't want to risk upsetting his wife and, through her, upsetting the children. "I'll still see the girls a lot while I'm at my folks' place," he said. I told him I hoped he was right. But it turned out he wasn't.

A few days later, a process server showed up at Bill's office and handed him the formal petition for divorce prepared by his wife's attorney. Unless his wife changed her mind, which seemed extremely unlikely, Bill would have to ask the court for permission to move back into the house. "Even if you want to try that," I told him, "we won't be able to get a hearing in front of a judge for at least six weeks. That's how backed up the courts are."

By then, I told Bill, the judge would look at the case and say something like this:

"The dad is living with his parents, and he's doing all right. The kids are living with the mom, and they're all right. This tem-porary situation seems to be working. So why should we upset the applecart and change everything? It's working."

At this point, I told Bill, the only way a judge might order a dad back into the house would be if the dad could show that he, not the mom, was the primary caregiver for the kids, or that he was an equal partner with her in the parenting. But that didn't fly in this case, at least not on the face of it. Bill worked long and hard running his business, and Ellen stayed home and took care of the kids. It might not seem right and it might not seem fair, but by moving out on that Sunday night Bill basically surrendered to his wife and put her in the position of driving any settlement discussions. After all, she now had what he wanted: the kids.

Bill had to overcome the fact that the kids could get along just fine without him. The less she let him see the kids, the stronger her case would be for persuading the court to award her primary custody. Despite Bill's efforts to see them almost every day, Ellen was making them available only once or twice a week, usually only for an hour or two due to alleged schedules, homework, and other activities. She was putting herself in position to argue that she was taking care of the children full-time, and they were doing well. Furthermore, she could argue that she couldn't get a job because the kids needed her at home, and consequently Bill should pay more financial support. If Bill argued that he loved the kids and wanted to be with them as much as possible and wanted to support them himself instead of giving her the money to do it, Ellen would have one short, powerful argument: "He moved out and left us."

In 99 out of 100 cases comparable to Bill's, he probably wouldn't be able to get a court to agree to give him primary custody. I told him that, but he insisted on asking for it, even though his wife wanted primary custody and was offering Bill the girls only one evening a week and every other weekend. At a minimum Bill wanted a 50-50 custody arrangement: The girls would stay a week with their mother and a week with him. He'd gotten a new place near the girls' school. They would have their own rooms. He didn't want to take the girls away from their mother; he simply wanted to continue to be as involved in their lives as he had been before the breakup. My firm agreed: If that's what Bill wanted, we'd try to get it for him, despite the long odds.

The deeper we got into the case, the more hopeful I became, even though Bill had moved out. Nobody disputed that Bill had spent a lot of time with his kids. Their teachers knew him and liked him. Parents and neighbors knew how involved he was. Meanwhile, we learned that his wife had been having an affair. That fact alone wouldn't necessarily affect a judge's custody considerations, but a new romance is sometimes a distraction. We looked for evidence that Ellen was spending more time with her new man and less time with her daughters.

Most divorces settle before trial. The two sides and their attorneys, no matter how bitter the feelings, usually manage to work out custody, financial, and other details of the agreement without asking the judge to hear the witnesses, consider the evidence, and decide the case. There was not going to be any settlement in this case, however, not as long as Bill pushed for shared custody and Ellen said no. The case I presented showed Bill to be a good provider and a good dad whose problem was that he had married a woman who fell out of love with him. We presented a range of evidence to back that up, highlighted by the testimony of one of the kids' teachers, who said Bill was one of the most involved and caring parents she had ever seen—mom or dad.

What decided the case, however, was Ellen's testimony. During her previous statements for the record, she had said that virtually all her expenses after she kicked Bill out had been to take care of the kids and the house. She insisted that she went out with friends—her girlfriends—only once every two weeks or so. On cross-examination, I presented her credit card bills. Those bills clearly showed that Ellen had been spending money almost every day—tennis lessons, shopping, spa treatments, and lunches that obviously were not at McDonald's. There were also a number of expenses from evening forays out for dinner and drinks. She sputtered in response, and the judge frowned at her. In her previous testimony, Ellen also said that she almost never—maybe once a month—asked her mother to keep the girls overnight. I called her mother as a rebuttal witness, and asked her how often she had been keeping the kids overnight. The grandma, not wanting to hurt her daughter but not wanting to commit perjury either, did her best to avoid answering.

"Oh, not that often," she said. "Every once in a while."

The evasive answers were probably more harmful to Ellen than if the grandma had simply told the truth and admitted that she kept the girls one or two nights a week.

The judge ruled in Bill's favor. He got 50-50 joint custody. He did not have to pay nearly as much child support as Ellen had been asking. She did not get nearly as much alimony as she had requested. And the judge told her to go out and get a job.

Bill was one of the few lucky guys who move out and don't suffer for it too much. If his wife hadn't mishandled her life and her divorce case, he would not have as much money in his bank account today or, more important, as much time with his daughters. They're teenagers now, and he has a strong relationship with both of them. He talks to his ex-wife only about issues concerning the kids, and he sees her only once in a while at school events.

In contrast, there's the example of Don, an executive with a pharmaceutical company. He had been in a long marriage—the kids were already teenagers—when he and his wife decided together to call it quits. She asked him to move out.

"There's no reason for me to move out of my own house," he said. "But if you want to move, go ahead."

"It's tense with you here," she said.

"I don't think so," he said.

She filed the divorce papers—Don was served them at home, while he was watching *Monday Night Football* down in the den—and he still didn't move out. Her lawyer started sending him certified letters, very official looking and officious sounding, proclaiming that he had to move out. He showed them to me, we had a laugh over them, stuck them in a file, and forgot about them.

"The kids are feeling the effects of you still being here while we are getting divorced," his wife told him.

"I don't think so," he said. The kids seemed fine, except when their mother tried to persuade them to ask him to move out. When that happened, they told her to quit bugging them.

Finally Don's wife went to court to get him out of the house. The judge seemed dumbfounded by the request. The man hadn't hurt anyone. He hadn't threatened anyone. He hadn't even raised his voice. He wasn't keeping his wife from doing anything she wanted to do. He was paying the bills. The kids didn't mind having him around.

"Compared with what I usually see," the judge said, "this doesn't even hit my radar screen. Request denied."

In the end, the wife's efforts to get the man out of the house probably hurt her settlement. Because the judge seemed to side with the husband, her lawyers ended up advising her to accept joint custody and a reduced financial package.

If Don had moved out, she would have had a much stronger case, and he very well may have had to pay her more while seeing less of the kids.

**DON'T MAKE A STUPID MISTAKE:
STAY IN THE HOME IF AT ALL POSSIBLE.**

CHOOSING THE WRONG LAWYER

WHEN A MAN goes to see a divorce lawyer, he is usually at the lowest point in his life. He is usually uncertain and confused. He may be angry. He is definitely under great stress. He could be in a state of emotional shock. When men sit down in front of me for the first time, quite a few of them seem like they are fighting back tears. A few can't help themselves and actually weep. Some say crazy stuff and are illogical and have trouble listening or absorbing what I am saying. Some curse and speak incredibly sharply about their wives. Even those trying to be calm and coherent often have difficulty carrying it off.

Sometimes the man has just learned that his wife wants a divorce. Sometimes he has just been served divorce papers, maybe out of the blue, a complete surprise. Sometimes his wife hasn't served papers yet, but he thinks she might. All the men who come to a divorce lawyer have two things in common. One, they have a big problem. Two, they want someone to take the problem off their hands.

In this chapter we'll look at when, where, and how to go about looking for the right law firm and lawyer. We'll look at the dangers of hiring a lawyer too quickly, and of waiting too long; what you should be looking for in a lawyer, and the questions to ask. We'll discuss the ways you can get the most out of your lawyer to get the best result from the divorce proceedings.

Too many men wait too long to start looking for a lawyer. I think it's because most men really don't want to get divorced. Even if they were guilty of some misconduct—an affair is one common example; a drinking problem is another—they want another chance. Even if their wives have told them in no uncertain terms that the marriage is over, many men hold out some faint hope that she will change her mind.

While they are waiting for another chance—a chance that may or may not come—they are wasting valuable time. More important, they are wasting their best chance to prepare for the case and to control it. Those two factors—preparation and control—are the biggest factors within your power to determine the outcome of your divorce case.

Men who wait are wasting their best chance to prepare for the case and to control it.

Too many men don't start looking for a lawyer until they have been served divorce papers. Then it's real. Then they absolutely have to do something about it. And they know that they have to do it right away. Consequently, they are running around as if their hair was on fire, looking to hire a lawyer, any lawyer, as soon as possible. First, they wait too long to start looking for a lawyer. Then they rush into hiring a lawyer too quickly—and it may not be the right lawyer for them or their case.

So when should you start looking for a lawyer? I think the search for a lawyer should commence the very second that the thought of divorce first occurs. Maybe that's not until the wife starts talking about a trial separation. Maybe it's the first time they have an argument and she says, "I can't live like this anymore." Maybe it's before she actually says or does anything. Maybe it's when he suspects she might have another man, or when he realizes that things simply aren't going well in the marriage, they're drifting apart, and they don't seem to have as much in common anymore.

Finding the right lawyer right away, before your wife has filed papers and even before she has announced she wants a divorce, is smart and gives you more options and alternatives. Whether or not your wife files for divorce, whether or not a divorce is actually going to happen, finding a lawyer at the first hint of the possibility of divorce gives you a chance to get the information and answers you need to be prepared for whatever develops. Your lawyer can advise you about getting your financial arrangements in order, along with all the pertinent tax records and other documents.

Finding a lawyer early in the process allows you and your lawyer to plan alternative strategies: what you should do if she tries to throw you out of the house, or if she says she is going to call the police, or if she takes off with the kids. If you suspect hanky-panky or financial misconduct, your lawyer can discuss with you hiring a private investigator or other options to help you find out for sure. You and your lawyer can develop a preliminary plan for your case, or a set of alternative plans to cover anticipated possibilities. If you find out your wife is going to file, you will be prepared for filing first (which is discussed in greater detail in Chapter 3). If she files before you do, you'll be prepared to respond quickly.

AUDITIONING ATTORNEYS

There's no set number of law firms you should check out, no maximum number of lawyers you need to interview. But I'd say your goal should be to sit down and talk to at least three different lawyers, and you might check out a dozen or more law firms before you decide which three lawyers to interview. This might seem like a lot of research, but these are steps you need to take if you want to find the best lawyer and law firm for you.

Finding the right law firm and lawyer should be a gut decision. You don't want to choose someone out of fear, panic, or desperation. You want to feel that your choice is the right person to help you. You want the right fit with your goals and perspectives. It's great if you get that feeling from the first lawyer you meet, but don't stop interviewing. Go see the other two or three or however many lawyers are on your list. You owe it to yourself to stick to your plan and gather more information. Besides, you never know. Maybe that second or third lawyer is an even better fit, and gives you an even better gut feeling.

In fact, I routinely encourage prospective clients to take initial consultations with other lawyers. "You don't need to decide right now," I tell them. "We will be available for you when you are ready to retain a firm. Do your research." This may seem crazy, but I am confident about the quality of work that our firm does and I want every client to be confident, too. I want a client to write that retainer check not out of fear, panic, or desperation, but because of his gut feeling that we're the right match.

HERE IS A RULE. Do not, I repeat, do not immediately hire the first lawyer you see. Too many men wait too long to start looking. A man gets slapped with divorce papers and calls up a buddy who was recently divorced. "Who'd you use?" the man asks. He gets the lawyer's name and phone number, and little or nothing else. The man calls and makes the first available appointment for an initial consultation—ideally it's within a day or two. In the office, he sits there, a bundle of emotions ranging from anger to fear with a lot in between, and hopes the lawyer will take his case. He hasn't done any research. He hasn't asked anyone else about the lawyer. He may not even have asked the buddy who just got divorced whether this lawyer did a good job. If the lawyer agrees to take the case—and it is rare that a lawyer won't—the man writes a retainer check and puts his fate in the hands of someone he knows little or nothing about.

Let's start at the beginning. The thought of divorce has first flickered across your mind. Your first urge is to call any friends who were recently divorced. It's a good place to start. But don't merely ask for contact information. Ask, "How was it to work with that lawyer?" The responses to this question can range from the unhelpful answer—OK, I guess—to insights that can lead you to ask more questions and get more details, such as the following:

"How did you find that lawyer? How many lawyers did you talk to before you hired that one?" If the lawyer came highly recommended or the buddy did a lot of good research, this might be a lawyer worth checking out. If this lawyer was the first and only lawyer your friend went to see, definitely follow up with more questions about the service he received.

"Did you like that lawyer?" You don't have to embrace the lawyer like a brother, but there's no point in trying to work with someone you don't respect or don't find comfortable to work with. Sometimes a lawyer and client simply don't match up well in personality. A lawyer who has an extremely aggressive personal manner, for example, might not be the best match for a client who doesn't want to see himself portrayed to his family and friends in the same extremely aggressive manner. Even more likely, a lawyer may seem too laid-back when the client is looking for someone who will really push his case for him.

"Is that lawyer a solo practitioner or in a firm with other lawyers?" A lawyer who is in a firm is more likely to have a good support system—other lawyers to help address your particular issues and back up your primary counsel, as well as administrative assistants to coordinate schedules, make contacts, and keep the volumes of paper in order. Sole practitioners typically have to do a lot more themselves, and if they're concentrating on other cases, your case might fall between the cracks.

"Did it seem like that lawyer knows the law and is up-to-date with all the latest rulings?" The vast majority of lawyers do keep up with the latest developments, especially those who concentrate their practices to a limited area of the law. A generalist who also has to keep up with criminal law, real estate law, tax law, etc., is not as likely to know all the latest nuances and developments in family law. To draw upon the medical doctor comparison again, you wouldn't ask a general practitioner, your family doctor, to fix your bum knee. You'd go to an orthopedic surgeon who specializes in knees.

"Did that lawyer give you a good plan, with some alternatives?" A lawyer should offer a plan, and a backup plan, and a backup to the backup. That can make a challenging process a little less challenging. It can offer the client control and confidence.

"Did it seem like that lawyer really cared about you and your case?" Another big complaint about their lawyers by men going through divorce is that the lawyer treated him just like any other client, and the case just like any other case. Your lawyer should give you full and undivided attention when you need it, and should be willing to do whatever is necessary to get you the best result possible.

"Was that attorney available and responsive? Did that attorney return your phone calls and e-mails right away?" Lack of communication is the No. 1 complaint from clients about their lawyers during divorce proceedings. You need a lawyer who will promise to stay in touch and be responsive, and who will keep that promise. Unlike many other areas of the law, divorce proceedings involve day-to-day issues that require a commitment from your lawyer to be available to answer questions and advise you on issues, even on evenings and weekends, if necessary.

> *Divorce proceedings involve day-to-day issues that require a commitment from your lawyer to be available to answer questions and advise you on issues, even on evenings and weekends, if necessary.*

"Was that lawyer ready to go to trial? Or did it seem like that lawyer wanted you to settle the case quickly?" Too many lawyers, unfortunately, simply want to clear cases. They focus on wrapping up a case, getting paid, and moving on to the next case. If you have a lawyer who is not willing to prepare to go to trial at the same time as pursuing settlement, you're bargaining from a position of weakness. You're going into battle with one arm tied behind your back.

"In depositions or court appearances, did that lawyer seem prepared and organized?" This is another big complaint among men going through divorce. Did the lawyer appear to have all the relevant documents? Were the exhibits in order? Was the lawyer on time for everything? Did the lawyer do everything he or she promised, and on time? How did the lawyer look? Some extremely competent lawyers look as rumpled as an unmade bed, but you've got to be sure that isn't going to hurt the judge's perception of you and your case.

"How did that lawyer charge you? How much was the initial

consultation? How much does that lawyer charge per hour? What did you have to pay up front for a retainer? Did you get regular billing statements to keep track of what you were being charged? How much did you end up paying altogether in legal fees?" We'll discuss fees, along with these other questions, in greater detail below. But money is a big part of the equation, and now is the time to start thinking about it.

And the final question to your friend: "Would you hire that lawyer if you could go back and do it all over again?" If a friend says he should have looked around a little more, it doesn't mean you shouldn't go talk to his lawyer or end up hiring his lawyer. It means you should look around beforehand.

Those are all questions you should ask your divorced friend about his lawyer. The more questions you can ask him, the better. But don't be misled. This is not all the research you need to do to find the right lawyer. Let's look at some of the other things you can do to identify lawyers you might want to talk to, and then the questions you might ask them, and the things you want to look for.

In developing a list of law firms and attorneys to interview, the first step would be to talk to as many friends as you can about their divorces and their lawyers. Talk to them all, without prying. Take a lot of what they say with a grain of salt; they almost certainly will not tell you everything, but that's okay because you don't want to know everything. Most men who have been through divorce still find it painful to talk about, even years later. But they also know what you're going through, and they're usually willing to help a brother out. Beyond friends, extend the circle of inquiries to acquaintances who may have interacted with divorce attorneys either professionally or personally: members of the clergy, counselors, financial professionals, or businesspeople you know and respect.

Do you know any lawyers? Perhaps a neighbor or fellow member of a social organization is a lawyer or judge. Maybe you have used a lawyer for other matters or you know a lawyer who has handled a relative's legal matters. Maybe you don't know any lawyers, but your financial advisor, real estate agent, banker, or health care provider probably has a law firm or lawyer for their business. Ask them to make an introduction to the lawyer, and then ask the lawyer for recommendations for <u>divorce lawyers.</u> When you do talk to a lawyer for references for other lawyers who do divorces, be aware that some states allow lawyers to take referral fees: If they recommend a client to another lawyer, the second lawyer pays the first lawyer what amounts to a finder's fee. If you ask a lawyer for only one name, you'll probably get the name of a lawyer who pays referral fees.

When you ask for referrals, put it this way: "Who are the three best divorce lawyers in town?" Or, "If you were getting a divorce, who would you ask to represent you?" Other questions to ask when you get a name: "<u>What is that lawyer's reputation among other lawyers? How is that lawyer regarded in the legal community?</u>"

In addition to personal contacts, you can also look at ads for lawyers: on TV, in the newspaper, in the Yellow Pages, and on websites. You can use Google, Bing, Yahoo!, or other Internet search tools to find divorce lawyers in your area. In many states lawyers aren't allowed to advertise their specialties, so it might be futile to look for ads for a lawyer claiming to be a specialist in divorce law. Sometimes, however, lawyers who

Look for code words such as "Men's Rights" or "Father's Rights."

"concentrate" or limit their practice are listed under "Family Law" and "Domestic Relations." In the ads, look for code words such as "Men's Rights" or "Father's Rights."

State, county, and local bar associations also often have listings of lawyers by areas of practice. Some bar associations or attorney licensing boards have listings for ethics violations or other complaints that have been filed against individual attorneys; it's worth it to see if there are such listings in your area, and whether a lawyer you are considering has been the target of complaints from previous clients.

I WOULD ADVISE against even talking to any lawyer who does not exclusively handle divorce and family-law cases. Yes, the lawyer who handled your late mother's estate may have done a good job and seem trustworthy. Maybe he or she has been your family's lawyer for decades. Maybe he even looks a little like Sam Waterston, the *Law & Order* actor who is probably TV's best-known lawyer in recent years. None of that should matter. You need someone whose entire practice is family law, someone who lives and breathes these cases every day, who knows the way local judges handle divorce cases, and who is up-to-date on all the latest twists and turns in the law. A lawyer who does wills and real estate closings and the occasional personal-injury lawsuit—not to mention the divorces for the clients he represents on all those other legal matters—has to keep up on all those different aspects of law. That's a tall order.

Priorities can also be an issue for the lawyer who takes different types of cases. Let's say a lawyer is working on three cases: a criminal case where the defendant could go to prison for 20 years if the lawyer loses the case; a personal-injury case where the lawyer could win damages of up to $1 million—and thereby a contingency fee of $250,000; and your divorce. Which one of those cases is most likely to get shifted to the back burner?

I would, if possible, also try to narrow the list of lawyers to interview down to family-law practitioners who primarily represent men, or who at least represent a fair number of men. Most divorce lawyers can and do offer perfectly adequate representation to either husbands or wives. But some lawyers, both male and female, focus on one gender or the other. Perhaps their personal sympathies lie more with one than the other, but more likely they simply know one perspective of the law better than the other.

Sometimes a man will come to our firm and talk to one of our male lawyers and ask, "Would it be better if a woman represented me?" Usually we say it probably wouldn't make a difference, but sometimes it might. Then we match the prospective client with one of several women lawyers on our staff. Our firm, Cordell & Cordell, has a long history of having women lawyers on staff to represent men in divorce cases. In fact, the other Cordell is my wife Yvonne, one of the finest family-law attorneys I've ever known. Having a woman lawyer usually doesn't make a difference, but I've got to say, I really do think it provides a subtle psychological edge in court—especially if the divorce trial is in front of a jury. It's unspoken, but the message is that maybe this man isn't so bad if he has at least one woman on his side.

One of our women lawyers recently had a case in the Midwest representing a journalist from Qatar, a tiny nation in the Middle East. His wife sued him for divorce in Missouri, and part of her case seemed to be that all Muslim men from the Middle East are controlling, abusive, sexist pigs. Simply having a woman attorney ask the questions at a pretrial deposition made a difference, our lawyer said, because wives in divorce proceedings seem to speak to her differently than male lawyers. "Women often try to get me on their side," she told me. "They take the attitude of, 'Well, you're a woman, so you know what it's like.' Or, 'You're a working mom, so you know what I mean.' The barriers come down, and they try for a level of familiarity that lets me get more information from them at depositions—information that I can use to help my client when we go to trial."

COST-ANALYZING AN ATTORNEY

Before we talk about the questions you want to ask the lawyers you interview, let's talk about money. Specifically, legal fees, beginning with the initial consultation. Too many men look for lawyers who don't charge for an initial consultation. Many men want free information and free advice. They want to find a lawyer without having to spend any money. That's a big mistake. True, some lawyers don't charge for an initial consultation. But the lawyers in our firm do, <u>and most good lawyers in solid firms do</u>. Our time and our advice are simply too valuable to give away. We think the initial consultation really is one of those times in life when you get what you pay for. If you want to talk to a lawyer who has enough free time to give away an hour of expertise, go ahead. But make sure you still talk to at least three other lawyers who do charge for an initial consultation. Spending that couple hundred bucks is a small price to pay for finding the right lawyer, and a mere drop in the bucket in terms of what finding the right lawyer can save you in the future.

Probably the most obvious question to ask a lawyer is, "How much do you charge?" Some lawyers will name a set price for the entire case, and it's usually a remarkably low price, maybe just a few hundred dollars plus court fees. "You have a pretty basic, straightforward case," they'll say. The client, of course, likes the idea that he has an uncomplicated case, and loves the idea of getting off cheaply on the legal fees.

LAWYERS WORKING FOR a set fee are going to get paid no matter how hard they work on the case, no matter how many hours they put in. Put yourself in their shoes. If you're going to be paid the same for a day's work, no matter whether you work nine hours or seven hours, how long are you going to work? For another thing, no legal case—and especially no divorce—ever turns out to be as simple and as uncomplicated as either the client or the lawyer hopes it will be. The lawyer who charges a lowball all-inclusive fee is probably relying on a handful of standard forms. The lawyer knows how to fill out those forms and where to file them. What if your case suddenly becomes a square peg and doesn't fit into the round hole of the lawyer's standard forms? Maybe the lawyer knows what to do, maybe not. Far too many clients who have tried to do their divorces cheaply have ended up going to another lawyer, one who charges much more and by the hour, to straighten out the mess. By the time it's all over, they've ended up paying more than if they had gone to the higher-priced lawyer in the first place.

By all means, try to get a handle on what you're going to pay in legal fees. How much are the hourly rates of the professionals who will be involved in your case, not just the primary lawyer but also the associate lawyers and legal assistants? Ask, "Why are your fees more than those charged by the law firm down the street?" Lawyers, like pretty much everyone else offering professional services, charge what they can. Lawyers who have more experience, knowledge, contacts, and records of success will charge more than younger, less experienced, less successful lawyers. Some lawyers charge higher rates for going to court than for other work, and that higher courtroom rate can add up.

In addition to the hourly fee, ask how much you have to put down as a retainer to hire the lawyer and how that retainer is handled. The retainer will usually be a refundable down payment that goes against the fees and expenses in your case. Fees and retainers vary widely from state to state, city to city, firm to firm, lawyer to lawyer. In most of the country, be prepared to pay a good divorce lawyer $200–$300 an hour and to put down a retainer of $2,000–$5,000 (or more per hour and a larger retainer, depending upon the community and the complexity of your case). That will get you eight to ten hours of the attorney's time—which is usually charged out in segments of 10 or 15 minutes. If your lawyer charges $300 an hour and bills by the quarter-hour, you're going to pay $75 for a short phone call to the lawyer. Incidentally, that's one of the quickest ways to run up your legal fees—call your lawyer every day just to find out if there is any news. If you have selected a dedicated divorce attorney, you will hear from your attorney regularly and immediately as soon as there are developments; you won't need to incur fees just to find out there are no developments in your case.

You'll also want to know when you will be billed and required to pay your fees or additional retainer as the case goes on and as the lawyer's hours pile up. Divorce cases involve substantial initial activity—and therefore fees—to address the information-gathering and temporary issues. Ongoing conflicts with the custody, visitation, or financial issues can add to the fees. Finally, the trial can be one day or several days, at six to ten hours per court day. Make sure your lawyer will bill you regularly, such as once a month. If you are not billed regularly, you cannot track the time and expense involved in pursuing your issues to help evaluate how your case is progressing and what you attorney is doing on your behalf.

There's no reason, obviously, to hire a lawyer who charges $300 an hour if you are convinced that a lawyer who charges $200 will do a better job. But if you think the higher-priced lawyer will do even a slightly better job, or has even a very small advantage over the less expensive lawyer, then you should probably bite the bullet and sign on for $300 an hour. It's important to look not only at the hourly fee, but at what you get for that. What's included? Will you have your lawyer's after-hours number or e-mail with a commitment to respond to you for those urgent issues that arise in custody and property matters? Is the lawyer available to meet in person or on the phone when your work schedule permits? Does the law firm provide copies of all documents in your case promptly to allow you to stay ahead of your wife on the information curve—by e-mail if you prefer? Some lawyers and law firms provide you, for little or no additional money, with a raft of resources and information aimed at helping you understand the process and empower you to help direct your case: books, pamphlets, websites, podcasts, workshops, etc. Or does the quoted rate only get you the minimum legal support during what is one of the most, if not the most, critical times in your life?

In addition, some lawyers and firms have associate attorneys, paralegals, and researchers who are qualified to do some of the work on your case, but for less money than the primary, more experienced lawyer would charge. Let's say, for example, that one man hires a solo practitioner who charges $250 an hour.

Another man hires an experienced lawyer who charges $300 an hour but has other staff in the firm who will do a lot of the case-work for $100–$200 an hour. That means you're paying $300 an hour for the time when that experienced lawyer is focusing on your case—meeting with you, planning strategy, taking de-positions, appearing at trial, and so on—with the support team doing other portions of the case at their lower rates. Meanwhile, the solo practitioner who charges $250 an hour is going to be doing all of the work and charging the same hourly rate whether appearing in court or doing simple paperwork.

Ask every lawyer for an estimate of how long your case will take, how many hours the lawyer will spend on it, and what your total, final cost will be. Experienced divorce lawyers won't give you a hard number—and they shouldn't. The time and expense of your case is subject to how difficult your case is. However, lawyers should be able to give you a rough estimate, or per-haps a range. This is what it could cost, at minimum, if there are absolutely no complications. The lawyer can also give you a ballpark range for how even a few complications can bump up your bills. And if it turns into a real mess, well, who knows? Most lawyers will tell you what the typical client pays and will give you the typical range, from a few thousand dollars into the mid–five figures. Ask the lawyer what is the most he or she has ever charged a man for a divorce, and why that client ended up paying $80,000 or $100,000 or whatever astronomical figure it was. This will give you an idea of what kind of complications can come up, and how quickly such complications can add to your legal fees.

One final note on fees. You're the client. You're the customer. You're the one who is doing the hiring. The lawyer wants your case, and your business. When you are interviewing lawyers, trying to decide whether to hire them, remember that they are also interviewing you, and deciding whether to take your case. One bottom-line question looms for lawyers: If I take this case, will this man pay me? Far too often, for various reasons, men drag their feet in paying their legal fees in a divorce. If paying your legal fees is not a priority for you, can you expect your lawyer to make your case his or her highest priority? Lawyers will work with their clients in paying fees, within reason. If you're concerned about how you're going to pony up the legal fees, be up front about it and see if the lawyer will work with you on making payments as your income permits, investments mature, or funds are otherwise available. Ask if the firm takes credit cards, thereby conserving your cash for you to spend on your children or allowing you to pay off other priority debts as part of the case strategy.

WHEN YOU WALK into a lawyer's office for an initial consult, you're looking for communication: good, open lines of communication, back and forth, between the two of you.

Be wary of a lawyer who seems to be doing a sales job. Some lawyers want to take every case that walks through the door, and they will do and say whatever they can to get your case. "I'm gonna really fight hard for you," they vow. But then they're short on specifics. They talk about how great they are as lawyers, they drop the names of clients they've represented and judges | *Be wary of a lawyer who seems to be doing a sales job.* | they play golf with, and they make it sound as if your case is going to be a piece of cake. "We're gonna win this thing," they say. "We're gonna get you everything you want. Nah, it won't take that long. And it won't be that expensive. You won't need to worry about anything, because I'll take care of everything."

That's doubtful. Be very cautious about any attorney who promises wonderful things. You don't want a sales job. You want an open, frank, honest discussion—a conversation, really—about your case. You want to know what your potential problems might be, and the possible solutions. You want a good, honest assessment of the case. If a lawyer tells you there are no problems, that's a problem. One of the biggest mistakes clients make is to think that they are hiring an attorney to get results. Nobody can know what the results are going to be. You are hiring an attorney for quality representation. That's all you can ask for and all you can expect. You don't want a lawyer who promises to "win" a case because, in truth, nobody wins a divorce. You don't want a lawyer who promises to beat up or destroy or burn down your wife, because that's both unrealistic and unprofessional. That's not what the law is all about. The law is about unraveling a financial and contractual relationship. You want a lawyer who will do the best possible job for you. That might be good enough to get you the result you want. Or it might not. Every case has extraneous factors that may be beyond the control of the lawyer or the client. All you can do in hiring a lawyer is try to find the one who will put you in the best position to get the result you want.

Let's examine the key points of discussion when interviewing lawyers. Experience is a good place to start. Ask lawyers how long they've been practicing, and what kind of law they practice. How many clients and cases do they handle in a year? How many of those are divorces? How many divorces have they handled in their career? As we've said, you don't want a generalist, someone who practices different types of law. Ask lawyers how long they have been practicing family law exclusively, what kind of cases and clients they've had, and how those cases have come out. You don't merely want a "divorce attorney." You want a divorce attorney who has experience with the issues men face in divorce. How many of their clients are men? If you're seeking custody, ask how many of their clients have been men with custody issues. If you're a small businessman and the valuation of your business is going to be a big issue, ask lawyers what kind of experience they've had in business valuations. Zero in on their experiences in representing men—and fathers, particularly, if custody is one of your concerns—and listen closely to what they say about the differences between representing men and women in divorce proceedings.

Location, location, location. Or in legal terminology, venue, venue, venue. Ask lawyers where they have practiced, in what courts, and before which judges. Do they have anything to say about the differences in appearing in different courts or before different judges? Judges have more discretion in family law than in perhaps any other branch of the law, and the judge in your case can have a huge impact on your result. In baseball, every umpire calls balls and strikes a little differently. Similarly, some judges are known for giving the benefit of the doubt to the wife. Is the lawyer willing to seek a change of judge (venue) if warranted? Many lawyers are reluctant to try to get a case removed from a judge. They fear that judge may resent the implication of unfairness, and then that judge will give the lawyer a rougher ride in future cases. You want a lawyer who isn't afraid to risk that rougher ride if that's what is best for your case.

It's reasonable to ask lawyers how many divorces they have tried, particularly in states such as Georgia where jury trials are an option. What percentage of their cases are settled, and how many have gone to trial? How do they feel about settlements versus going to trial? This is important, because you don't want a lawyer who is reluctant to try the case. Far too many divorce lawyers want to settle cases out of court simply because it's easier for them. Going to trial is an incredible amount of work for a lawyer, and there's a lot of pressure in both preparation and performance. If a lawyer says he or she settles most cases, and tries to make that sound like a positive, don't believe it. Your wife's lawyer will know if your attorney is shy about going to court, and will push that advantage in the negotiations.

A lawyer who doesn't want to go to court is more likely to make concessions and then try to tell you, "This is the best deal we could get. It's not worth all the hassle of going to court." You've got to ask: Is it possible we'll get a better deal at trial? Even if you would rather settle than go to trial—and most men would, because going to trial is a lot of preparation and pressure for them, too—then the best way to force a settlement is to show that your case is strong enough to take to trial. You're dealing from strength rather than weakness, and confidence rather than fear.

"Part of my job," I sometimes tell clients, "is to make the other side worry—worry that they are going to lose something if we go to trial." Think about when you buy a car and you're negotiating with the salesperson. Your ultimate negotiating tool is the threat of walking away. "I don't need to buy the car today," you say, and start to walk away. That's what strikes fear in the salesperson—the fear of losing the sale—and leads to more compromise, a lower price, a better offer. The same thing happens in negotiations over a divorce settlement. If we are willing to go to trial and that makes the other side afraid they might lose the deal we are offering, they're more likely to take the deal.

My clients tell me one of the things they like best about our firm is our case management system. We have two administrative staffers who work as concierges, keeping track of cases and shepherding them along. Our clients get regular reports on what's happening with their cases. If one of my clients calls to confirm some deadlines or ask about his bill, he can talk to one of them instead of waiting for me to be available and charge them my professional fee for answering a simple non-law question. Even among our lawyers, however, we have a rule: All phone calls and e-mails must be answered within a day. Every client gets his lawyer's personal mobile phone number, and those phones are on from first thing in the morning until eight or nine o'clock in the evening.

THAT BRINGS US to communication, the number one complaint that clients have about their divorce attorneys. Too many clients say they never heard from their attorneys. They weren't even sure what their attorneys had done for them, if anything. They weren't told exactly how the process works, step by step. They weren't advised of their options, and they weren't offered any alternatives. All they heard from the lawyers, usually right on the deadline, was, "You have to do this." They felt helpless.

Lack of communication is the number one complaint that clients have about their divorce attorneys.

Good communication should begin at the initial consultation, when you first meet and interview a lawyer. Remember, communication has to be a two-way street. You need to clearly express your goals and expectations—what you want from the case. Listen carefully to what the lawyer says is reasonable to expect in terms of results. Don't anticipate that just because your buddy got a divorce and is paying $1,000 a month child support that you're going to pay $1,000 a month child support, too. The facts of every case are different. Explain your facts clearly and simply. If telling stories is the best way for you to communicate, tell your stories. Start at the beginning. Tell your story, and the story of you and your wife as a couple. If you have kids, tell the story of your family. The lawyer may be an expert in the law, but you are the expert on your life—on what has gone right and what has gone wrong, and the lawyer needs to know what you know.

Don't go overboard, of course. Time is money, for both you and the lawyer. The lawyer doesn't need to know what kind of toothpaste you use or what books you're reading—unless that information is pertinent to the case. As you talk, think about how you feel in talking to the lawyer. Is he or she easy to talk to? This is an extremely emotional time, and you've got to be brutally honest about yourself. You may also need to be totally open about things that you never imagined you would discuss with a stranger. You've got to be able to talk about the most intimate details of your marriage with your lawyer. You've got to be able to spill your guts.

You aren't hiring a lawyer simply to perform a service, the way you would hire a plumber to fix your leaky pipes. You're hiring a partner, someone with the expertise to steer you. That's a good metaphor. You're the captain of your ship, and the lawyer is the harbor pilot who comes out in a tugboat for a brief time to help guide your ship over the shoals as you enter the harbor. The more the harbor pilot knows about you and your ship, the better and safer the route you take.

Right from that initial consultation, lawyers should be able to give you a tutorial on how the wheels of justice will grind through your case. How does the system work? What happens first? What happens next? When do I get to see my kids? Do I have to pay her any money now? When will all this be over? Ask the attorney for an estimated timeline for settlement and trial. Ask for worse-case and best-case scenarios. Ask not only what is possible—sure, zero custody is always one possibility and full custody is always another—but what the lawyer thinks is probable. Ask for a plan. How does the lawyer foresee the case unfolding? What are the most likely points where things could go wrong? If things go wrong, what alternatives can the lawyer present for responding and carrying on? The plan may change as the case unfolds, but from that first meeting the lawyer you are going to hire should be able to clearly lay out the plan for handling your case.

DON'T MAKE A STUPID MISTAKE: CHECK OUT SEVERAL LAWYERS TO FIND THE RIGHT PARTNER FOR YOUR CASE.

A CHECKLIST OF QUESTIONS WHEN INTERVIEWING A LAWYER

✓ How long have you been practicing? Are you a specialist in divorce and family law? Do you handle divorce and family-law cases exclusively? How many divorce cases have you handled? How many last year? Do you have any special certification or training in family law?

✓ Are you comfortable representing men in divorce? How many men have you represented? Are you representing any men right now? What are the special problems or issues or concerns for men in divorce? Would you mind giving me a couple of your recent male clients for referrals?

✓ Do you work alone? What kind of legal and administrative support do you have? Will I also be working with other lawyers, paralegals, and other staff in your office?

✓ Where will my case be heard? Are you familiar with that court and those judges?

✓ From what I've told you about my case, what are your thoughts on how you'd handle it? What are the key points in the case, the pivotal issues?

✓ What can we do in terms of strategy and tactics for helping me get what I want?

✓ What are the chances of my getting what I want? What are the other possible results and how likely are they?

✓ How do you charge? How much do I have to put down in advance as a retainer? How much do you think the whole case will cost in legal fees—a ballpark figure or a broad range?

✓ Are you familiar with experts who might be called in on my case? How much might those expenses add to my legal fees?

✓ Overall, how long do you think my case will take? What's the time range?

✓ How will you keep me informed about the case? Will you give me regular progress reports? How often? By phone or e-mail? What's the best way for me to contact you or your staff?

✓ If I call you with a quick question, how much will that cost me? If I call a paralegal or someone else working on the case, will that cost less?

✓ How do you feel about going to trial in a divorce case? Do most of your cases settle out of court? How many of your cases went to trial last year? When was the last time you went to trial? What happened in that case?

✓ What's your general philosophy or approach when representing men in divorce cases?

WAITING FOR
YOUR WIFE TO
FILE

JACK SAT DOWN in front of me, his face in anguish, and started talking. He was from a blue-collar family. He went into the Army after high school, served in the first Gulf War back in the early 1990s, came back and went to college, worked for an auto dealership, and eventually bought out the owner. His auto dealership wasn't the biggest one in the area, but not the smallest, either. He made a decent living, but wasn't rich. His wife stayed home with their three kids, two in grade school and one in middle school. He didn't think she had anyone else, but he didn't know for sure. Things had been bad between them for a while, and had been growing worse lately. They just didn't seem to agree on anything—money, kids, anything. They had been spending less and less time together. But it was still a surprise to him when she announced two nights earlier, after the kids had gone to bed, that they should split up.

I questioned Jack closely. No, his wife didn't have a lawyer yet, but was looking for one. No, she didn't seem like she was going to change her mind. Maybe they could reconcile some-day, but she seemed determined to file for divorce now. He had moved into the guest room. Yes, things were tense, but he and his wife were not openly bickering or sniping at each other. They were keeping up appearances for the kids' sake.

Jack agreed to hire my firm, and I agreed that we would represent him.

"What should I do?" he said. "I have no idea what to do first."

"Jack, you've already done the first two things, and you've done them well," I said. "You stayed in the house and you got a lawyer. Now there's one more thing you should think about doing right now."

"What's that?" he asked.

"File first," I said. "Let's get our ducks in a row and beat her to the punch. You be the one, instead of her, to file for the divorce."

> *File first. Let's get our ducks in a row and beat her to the punch. You be the one, instead of her, to file for the divorce.*

Jack was shocked, as so many men are when they hear that very solid piece of advice. It wasn't what he expected. It wasn't how he thought his divorce would play out. He wasn't the one who was initiating the divorce, she was. He didn't want it to look like he was a bad man or that splitting up was his idea.

I explained to him, as my lawyers have explained to thousands of men, why it is advantageous—and often crucial—to be the one to file for the divorce. There are legal advantages, both in and out of court, whether the divorce agreement is settled or whether it goes to trial. Filing first can give him better terms from the very start, when the judge issues temporary orders setting the financial support and custody arrangements while the divorce is pending. Filing first can also mean a better deal for the dad in the final divorce decree.

"I am representing you right here and now, the man sitting in front of me today," I told Jack. "But I am also representing the man you will be three years from today. You're going to be a lot different. You're not going to be married anymore, for one thing. The terms of the divorce are going to matter a great deal in determining what your life is like when you're single again— or what life is like for you and your new wife if you get married again. The terms of the divorce will determine how much money you have in the future. The terms will determine how much time you spend with your kids, and that determines what kind of relationship you will have with them. I want you to consider filing first because you will have a better chance of getting a favorable divorce decree."

Jack seemed dubious.

"Look," I said. "You were in the Army, right? I don't want to paint your wife as the enemy, or divorce as a war. It doesn't need to be like that. But this is a contest that is going to be fought in the judicial system. It's a legal battle between two sides. Now, do you want to give the other side the advantage of choosing the time and place for the battle to begin? Or do you want to choose? Do you want to let her file first, and then you'll react? If so, you'll be on the defensive not only at the start, but throughout the proceedings. Or do you want to take the initiative? Would you rather play offense or defense?"

THE RACE TO THE COURTHOUSE

Historically across much of America, divorce proceedings often began with a "race to the courthouse." When a couple decided to divorce, they would race—sometimes literally—to be the first to file a petition for divorce. This was because of the huge advantages in many jurisdictions for the plaintiff—the person who filed first. In effect, the mere filing by one party would "freeze" the situation, like a snapshot. The wife could not empty the bank accounts, the husband could not take the kids to live with him, and nobody could do anything to alter the physical, financial, or family relationship without subsequent permission from the courts.

It is much more common now for that "snapshot" to freeze the situation after an initial court hearing to decide the temporary orders. A judge typically hears evidence from both sides and then issues temporary orders that lay down the rules during the proceedings. The judge decides who gets the kids when, who can live in the house, who pays how much financial support to the other, and so on. In theory, it doesn't matter who files first. Both sides are supposed to get a fair hearing when the judge determines the temporary orders.

That's the theory: There's no advantage to filing first. But theory is different from practice. In real life, it can make a huge strategic difference if you file first.

"For one thing," we tell clients, "the sooner you file, the less time you give her to prepare: the less time to gather her documents, the less time to look through your documents, the less time to build a case against you, the less time for her to hit your joint accounts and grab the money."

We had that happen to one man who came to us. Mike was

a stay-at-home dad. His wife was a high-powered executive for a pharmaceutical company. They had two kids, ages four and seven. He had stayed home with them ever since the first one was born. He'd had a decent career as a pharmaceutical sales rep, but when he and his wife decided to start a family, they agreed that one of them should stay home. She had the better job, and he was better suited to staying home and taking care of the kids, so it was a no-brainer. He was Mr. Mom and she was Ms. Breadwinner.

When she declared that she was leaving him for someone "more exciting," Mike was devastated. "More exciting than the man who is raising her kids?" he wondered. He tried to talk her out of it, to give the marriage another try, but she was adamant. They were through. So Mike came to us. Leaving the house was not an issue with him because she had packed up and left. He was in the house with the kids.

We urged Mike to let us file the divorce petition right away. He said no. He didn't want to split up, and he didn't want to do anything that made it look like he wanted to split up.

We pointed out that pretty much everything they had was in her name. Yes, he had his own retirement account, and they had a small joint checking account for minor household expenses, but everything else—their main savings account, her bigger checking account for paying major bills such as the mortgage and utilities and credit card bills, her much bigger retirement account, and their investment account—were all in her name. Even the house was in her name. "What if she stops paying the bills?" we asked.

"No way," Mike said. "She'd never do that to me."

Well, she did. Not only did she stop paying the bills she usually paid from her account, she looted the joint checking account for paying household expenses. Mike wrote a check for groceries, it bounced, and he found she had left only $10 in the account. He had to dip into his retirement account to pay the household expenses. That continued until after he finally filed for divorce a few days later and we were able to get in front of a judge for temporary orders a couple of weeks later. Yes, the judge issued temporary orders for Mike's wife to resume paying the bills, but in the meantime he had significantly diminished his retirement account—and would pay the penalties at tax time. Maybe we'd get some of that money back in the final settlement, but maybe not. Mike would have been a lot better off if he had filed for divorce right away and taken at least half of the money that was in the joint account for household expenses. In fact, thinking about it, we might have counseled that he take it all; it was for household expenses and she had already left the household.

"In one respect you're lucky," we told Mike. "What if she had wanted the kids? She's got the resources; she could have just taken the kids and moved them somewhere else. Then you'd be in court arguing not only for money, but for your kids."

Another reason to file first is to avoid giving the wife the chance to allege mistreatment. If she files first, she can go straight to the judge and ask that the man be barred from the house. This is called an ex parte order when it is made on the say-so of just one of the parties. It is not unusual: The wife files for divorce, and at the same time claims that her husband is beating her or threatening her or mistreating the children. Naturally, courts are cautious and careful about this. If a woman says she feels threatened, the courts are likely to take her word for it, at least until the husband can get there to present his side of it.

We had this happen to one of our clients recently. We advised him to file first, and he refused. So she filed, and when she did her lawyer told the judge that she was afraid her husband was going to be so angry about it that he would beat her up. The judge sent two cops to her husband's workplace. They escorted him home and gave him 20 minutes to pack his stuff up. He never set foot in that house again.

But if the man files first, that's a different story. One man, a construction worker nicknamed Red, came to us and said, "My wife is going to file for divorce, and I think she is going to say she's afraid I'm going to hit her."

"Okay," we replied. "Has she ever called the police before? Have you ever hit her? Are you going to hit her? What if she makes you so crazy with this divorce talk that you do hit her? What if she taunts you and prods you and makes you hit her?"

"No," Red said. "The police have never been to our house. I've never laid a hand on her, or any other woman. The kids, either. I haven't hit anybody since I was in a fight after school in second grade. That's not me."

"Good," we said. "Let's file right away."

We explained that if we filed for divorce first, it would be much more difficult for Red's wife to get an ex parte hearing. It would be more difficult for her to get a judge to issue temporary orders that would keep him out of the house or away from the kids.

"It's not a legal issue," we told Red. "It's common sense: If she was so afraid of you, why did she wait till you filed for divorce to complain? In fact, if things were so bad, why didn't she file for divorce first?"

We've seen countless examples where the wife loses—accidentally, of course—financial records the man has left behind. If you move quickly, file first, and don't give her a chance to hide or "lose" those records, you save yourself a lot of time and trouble and lawyer's fees for chasing down those "lost" documents.

Sometimes the advantage in filing first, as any number of classic texts about real military battles agree, comes from surprise. She intends to file for divorce. She never anticipates that her husband—the poor schmuck—will file first. We've taken advantage of that attitude many times. For example, the man comes in all upset and says, "My wife is having an affair, and I think she's gonna leave me."

"Are you sure?" we ask. "Are you sure she's having an affair, and are you sure she's going to leave you?"

He's sure about both, but he doesn't have any proof she's having an affair.

Fine, we say, let's go out and get some proof. In a few cases, we've helped our client hire a private investigator to come up with the evidence, usually records of meetings with the boyfriend in bars or motels or at his place. We don't go for the sordid, graphic "Gotcha!" photos that you see in movies. But we provide eyewitness and documentary proof that neither the soon-to-be-ex-wife nor the boyfriend can dispute.

When we have that evidence, we have one word for our client: File. Go to court, file for divorce, and don't give her a chance to lose the boyfriend. Too often a suspicious husband confronts his wife, accuses her of having a boyfriend, they argue, and she recognizes that she's going to get a divorce. So she tells the boyfriend they have to chill for a while, till she gets an attorney and gets all the documents lined up. There's no chance for the husband to gather evidence of the affair. If you, as the husband who has been cheated on, can beat her to the punch, you're going to have a much stronger case—including that evidence of an affair—than if you sit back and wait for her to file. Play offense, not defense.

Once in a while health considerations—real or imagined—are

a factor for a man facing divorce. For example, we had a case where the man came in, his wife wanted a divorce, and he was happy to give her one. "She's crazy," he said. "Not just a little crazy. I mean really crazy—certifiable." Among his wife's various syndromes and conditions was hypochondria. Even in the best of times she was always running to doctors with one symptom or another. When things got stressful and when she was under pressure—as she no doubt would be during a divorce—she went to the doctor even more. If she couldn't get a diagnosis she wanted or the medication she thought she needed, she'd shop around, going from doctor to doctor, specialist to specialist. We advised our client to file right away in order to minimize the amount he would have to pay to support her hypochondria. Later he told us, "You know, that was the single best piece of advice you gave me. If I had waited for her to file, she probably would have taken another three to six months to get around to it, and that would have meant another three to six months of me forking over for her co-payments and for all those medicines and treatments that insurance doesn't cover."

Geography can also be a factor. To a military commander, picking the place of the battle can be just as important as the timing. In legal proceedings, the location, or venue, of the case is just as important. If there's any reason to think your wife might file for divorce somewhere that is a disadvantage to you, or simply inconvenient, you should file first in the court where you want the proceedings to be held. This is often an issue for couples when one or both is in the military, and the divorce could be filed either in the county where one or both of them is based, or in the county where one of them is living with the kids while the other is away on duty, or the county where they both last lived together. It can get complicated. For a man whose wife files somewhere far away—maybe it's in a town he's never or rarely visited—it can be like playing an away game. He has to travel, he doesn't know the town, and he doesn't have any support network.

For instance, we had a client, Ralph, who was in the military in Georgia, where he had been living with his wife, Alice, and their only child. He was away on a training mission for a few days, and when he returned he found that she had moved back to her parents' house in Illinois with their daughter, and she had filed for divorce there.

"How am I going to do this?" Ralph asked us. "Do I need to get a lawyer in Illinois? Am I going to have to take time off and go back and forth? I can't afford plane tickets, and I can't afford the time off to drive back and forth . . ."

We counseled him to file for divorce in Georgia as soon as he could, which he did. Then, luckily, we were able to persuade the court in Illinois that the divorce should properly be heard in Georgia, where Ralph and Alice had lived together, rather than Illinois, where they never had lived. But if he hadn't moved quickly, and if her case had gotten a little farther in the Illinois courts, we might not have been able to bring it back to Georgia. As a footnote to that case, it turned out that Alice had been having an affair, and the courts in Georgia take that into consideration when awarding maintenance payments. The courts in Illinois don't. So by having the case adjudicated in Georgia, Alice was made to pay, literally, for her indiscretions.

Within a state, a lawyer might want to choose among different county, parish, or circuit courts. One of our clients, Stan, an EMT first responder, worked and lived in a county with a large urban population. He and his wife, Sara, had a one-year-old son. His wife found a new man and moved with the child back to her parents' home in a rural county. Sara's family was rooted in the smaller county, while Stan's was not; Sara thought that would give her a leg up in the custody case. Sara filed first in the rural county and obtained an unwarranted emergency order of protection by the time Stan came to us. Sara had retained one of the few local attorneys in the county seat. Her attorney was not a divorce attorney but a general practitioner, which is common in smaller court circuits. Instead of hiring another local lawyer, which would have locked the case into the small county where Sara's family had influence, Stan came to us. We were able to show that all the issues in the case—custody, finances, and her untrue allegations about Stan threatening her—were based in the larger county. We were able to get the case moved back to the larger county. Stan didn't suffer in the long run, but failing to file first cost him additional legal fees and the travel time and expenses going back and forth to the rural county during the early stages of the case.

THE ADVANTAGE OF PLAYING OFFENSE

When you actually get in front of a court, it's not supposed to matter who filed first. But it does. Here's the reason: In any hearing or trial, the side that files first puts on their case first. If you file, you speak first in court. That's huge. The side that presents first states its case. They're on offense. The side that presents second has to respond to what was said. They're on defense. It's human nature. If you have kids, you know what happens when two or more of them come to you with some complaint.

"My little brother hit me," the big sister reports.

You listen, gather the facts, and then turn to the little brother: "Did you do that? Why did you do that?"

Most of the time the little brother gets punished or scolded, and the big sister, the one who brought the complaint, skips away. But what if the little brother says, "Hey, she started it. She hit me first!"

Then you might go back to the big sister for more information. Maybe she has an excuse, maybe not. Maybe you believe her story, maybe you believe his story. Either way, the odds are that the little brother is still in trouble. He still gets punished or at least scolded: "If she hits you, don't hit her back. Come and tell me."

The same thing happens in court. If the man has done something wrong, or is going to be accused of doing something wrong, it is especially important for him to file first and present his case first in court, whether at a hearing to determine temporary orders or at a trial to determine the final terms of the divorce decree. It doesn't matter whether he's done it or not; filing first and presenting first is the best way to cover problems. The best defense is a good offense.

Let's say it's a typical case where the wife has filed first and is going to blame her husband's drinking for the breakup of the marriage. It happens all the time. She goes in front of the judge and gives chapter and verse. He came home drunk on their anniversary and forgot to give her a present. He had a few beers and yelled at the kids for nothing. He has wine with dinner every evening, and then goes to sleep on the couch watching TV. Maybe the wife cries on the stand about how his drinking has ruined her perfect life.

When the man finally has a chance to speak, the judge has heard only one side of the story, and it's not a very good side. The judge is looking at him like he's a really poor excuse for a husband. The man can sputter about how she drove him to drink, or how she's exaggerating about how much he drinks, or how she drinks just as much as he does. The man can say he's cut down or he's getting help. But the fact remains that he is responding to this woman's tearful complaints about how he has done her wrong.

Let's switch it around, reverse it. Let's say the man files for divorce first. When it comes time to go to court and the two parties and their lawyers walk into the courtroom, he's called on first to tell his story. He can talk about how the marriage has disintegrated over time, and how that has led him to drink more. Maybe he went out drinking on their anniversary because she had picked a fight with him that morning. Maybe he had learned that she had been spending too much money, and they didn't have enough cash to go out for an anniversary dinner. Maybe he falls asleep on the couch because it's less painful than her continual rejection of his affection. Maybe they share the bottle of wine at dinner every night.

Maybe—and this can be the strongest strategy of all—he tells the court worse things about himself than she would have. Maybe he says yeah, now I recognize that I was letting my marital problems get the best of me, and I was drinking too much, and it was affecting my relationship with my kids, but now I've quit drinking and I'm going to Alcoholics Anonymous meetings and I haven't had a drop in six weeks, Your Honor.

In the face of that, what is the wife going to say when it's her turn? If he's already told the world about his mistakes, what good does it do for her to add to that? It'll just look like she is piling on, like she's bitter, like she just wants to hurt him. To a judge, it may look like she is wasting the court's time by belaboring a point that's already been made.

Besides, she will feel obliged to answer the complaints the man made about her. Did she really pick fights with him? Did she really withhold affection? Is she really spending their joint funds irresponsibly? She's on defense instead of offense.

It's especially important for the man to file first if his misconduct is going to be part of the record. You better file first if you've committed adultery, have anger issues, mishandled your money, or you're a reformed substance abuser. If you're my client, I want my client on the stand at the very start, acknowledging all the things that he's done. And being repentant for them. Taking ownership of a problem yourself is a way to keep someone else from making it theirs and using it against you. Then you explain that the things that your wife is going to say aren't true, or are only partly true, or used to be true but you're doing something about it and changing your evil ways. Let me give you two cases to illustrate.

> *You better file first if you've committed adultery, have anger issues, mishandled your money, or you're a reformed substance abuser.*

Case No. 1: My client, Wayne, a printer, refused to file first. He wanted his wife, a stay-at-home mom, to file because he didn't want the divorce. So she took the stand first. And the entire first hour of the trial she testified about what a big drunk Wayne was. On and on. In fact, my client did drink beer every night. Sometimes he had a few too many and staggered around and said stupid things. Once in a while he threw up. A couple of times he passed out in the bathroom, hugging the porcelain, and she found him in the morning. "If he didn't drink we'd still be together," she said.

Because she had gone on and on, I had to spend a lot of time talking about Wayne's drinking, and how it really didn't matter in a legal sense and shouldn't really be affecting the outcome of the case. It shouldn't even have been part of the case. It was irrelevant. Their kids were grown and gone, so they weren't affected.

Nobody, not even the wife, who kept the books part-time in the print shop, said that the beer drinking affected Wayne's work.

It was stupid for the case to be centered on his beer drinking. But it was, simply because she had filed first and testified first. If I had been able to put Wayne on the stand first and dismissed the beer drinking as inconsequential and little more than one of her many pet peeves about him, it would have been a different story. Following her husband, she would have appeared petty and spiteful by continuing to harp on and on about his beer. We ended up with a decent result for Wayne, but it took a lot more hard work in court than if he had filed first.

Case No. 2: Norman was a salesman who had committed adultery—cheerfully and enthusiastically and apparently as often as he possibly could. He told me about it right away, and said his wife, a teacher, was going to use that as the reason for the divorce. He told me he had been carrying on with a woman in a nearby town for years, unbeknownst to his wife. She'd found out when Norman accidentally left a credit card statement lying around. "Yeah, I know," he said. "Bonehead move."

When the wife found the credit card statement, she threw a fit and told Norman she wanted a divorce. He was waiting in my office the next morning when I came in.

"I think she's gonna file the papers tomorrow," he said.

"Tomorrow?" I asked. "That's lucky." He looked puzzled. How could that be lucky?

"It's lucky," I explained, "because it gives you the chance to file today."

He did, and consequently he took the stand first. Yes, he had a girlfriend. No, he hadn't told his wife because he didn't want to hurt her. Yes, he wanted to divorce his wife and marry the girlfriend. But he wanted to wait until he was in a little better financial position so he could give his wife a better settlement.

"Actually," he testified, "our marriage has been over for a long time. I think we kind of divorced ourselves about ten years ago." He told the judge how they didn't sleep in the same bed, and hadn't for years. They didn't even sleep in the same room. No sex.

"We weren't friends," he testified. "We didn't do anything together. We each had an entirely separate set of friends. She drove me away. She stopped sleeping with me and stopped talking to me. We don't even spend time together. That's why I went out and got a girlfriend."

His testimony was powerful. Imagine if his wife had taken the stand first, crying about how she had been duped and he had cheated on her, and she had no idea, and it had been a perfect marriage up until then. Instead, she had to address his points, and answer them truthfully: No, they did not share a bed, and hadn't for years. No, she could not remember the last time the two of them went out and did something together.

Telling your side of the story first has nothing to do with the law. It is all about human nature. If you get your points on the record first, that can have a big influence on people, including judges. Sure, judges are trained in the law, but they're still human. In Norman's case, I have no doubt the wife would have cried if she had testified first. Instead, because he testified first, she was too busy defending and confirming and explaining his statements about the sham marriage. And yes, we got a fair result from the judge in that case.

In cases where the husband filed and testified first, I've seen women take the stand and then let loose with a whole stream of complaints about how rotten the man was. And I've heard judges ask, "Well, if things were so bad, why didn't you file for divorce?"

By filing first, you can be the one controlling the situation. The biggest issue is control of gathering information. That's largely what divorce litigation is about: getting and controlling information, especially about finances, and talking to witnesses and getting them on your side. The faster you can move, the better position you're going to be in. You can get a head start on gathering information and shaping the case by filing first, and then you can set the tone for the case by appearing first.

THE RULES AT the hearing for temporary orders, which ideally takes place within a few weeks of the divorce papers being filed, vary from state to state. In some states, the plaintiff—the person who files first—still has a big advantage from winning the race to the courthouse. If the plaintiff had custody of the children and sole possession of the house and control of most of the joint assets at the moment the papers were filed, that's the snapshot that is frozen until a judge says otherwise.

For a dad who didn't file first, this can be a disaster. The mom filed first, cleaned out the accounts, changed the locks so he couldn't get back in the house, and isn't letting him see the kids. He's supposed to wait till the hearing for temporary orders to try to get a fair shake. If he breaks into the house to get his clothes or loses his temper when pleading with her to let him have the kids for an afternoon, she can call the police. The police are going to come and find a broken window or an angry dad, and they're going to arrest him.

So that dad has to bide his time till the hearing; if he doesn't, he risks looking like a madman. But during those weeks that he's making nice and keeping his nose clean, the so-called temporary situation is becoming more permanent every day. Even if his lawyers get a hearing for him quickly—within a few days, or a week or two—by then there is a real chance the judge will look at him and say, "Okay, you've been out of the house, and you haven't seen your kids very much, and you haven't had access to the money that was in your joint accounts. But things seem to be working. You've still got a paycheck and you're paying your bills. You've found another place to stay. You haven't been complaining about not seeing the kids, and they haven't been complaining about not seeing you. Maybe we'll tweak things a little bit on the finances and the custody, but basically, let's leave things like they are in the temporary orders. If anything is unfair, it can be fixed in the final divorce decree."

Except that you can already see how "temporary" has a way of turning into "permanent" in the world of divorce. The fact that you have been out of the house and had only minimal contact with the kids and gotten along without much money for six months or a year shows that you can get by permanently. Again the judge can say, "If it's working, why should we change it?"

The biggest exception is on the custody issue when plaintiffs file for divorce and then grab the kids and run. They might have the advantage for a few weeks, until the temporary hearings. Judges almost always require them to bring the kids back and share custody, and often punish them by awarding joint or sole custody to the parent who was left behind.

In one recent case at our firm, the mother filed for divorce in the Midwest and headed to California with the couple's only child, who was only four months old at the time. The father, Gordon, our client, had been intending to file first, but she found out and beat him by a single day in the race to the courthouse.

Gordon was beside himself. "We're screwed," he moaned. "She filed first, and she took the baby and now I have to fight to get her back. We're on our heels. We're playing defense."

Our lawyer tried to reassure him. "No, we're not on our heels," she assured Gordon. "We're still in control of the situation because you've done everything right. You're not the one who ran away with the baby." We had Gordon call the police and report a kidnapping—not so much because we wanted the wife arrested (though that would have been okay with our client by then), but so the snatching and his objection was part of the public record when we got in front of a judge. Indeed, the effect of running away with the baby was much more significant. The judge made it clear to the wife's lawyer: Get her back here on the next plane, with the baby, or she would indeed be subject to arrest. She brought the baby back, and the judge ended up awarding Gordon everything we proposed in terms of both custody and financial support.

Speaking of judges, there's a lot of leeway in <u>family law</u>. Yes, there are rules and procedures, but there are also a lot of gray areas, a lot of judgment calls, and in pretty much every jurisdiction in America the buck stops with the judge. The judge has a lot of discretion.

Judges are human, and subject to the same biases and quirks and impatience as the rest of us. One of our lawyers tells an amazing story about the first time he appeared before a judge who had a reputation for, uh, shall we say, deciding the case rather quickly. Our lawyer thought the case might end up before this judge, so he instructed our client, a textile executive, to file first, and our client did. When it came time for the trial, we put on our client's case first, and the judge was intensely interested. He asked questions. He pored over the documents we put into evidence. He was extremely involved, engaged, and hands-on. After about a half hour, it seemed like he not only understood the case we were putting on—losing lawyers often complain afterward, "The judge didn't get it . . ."—but he was nodding in appreciation and agreement.

"My gosh, I think we've won this case already," our lawyer said to himself. And he was right. He wrapped up the case quickly, and turned the floor over to the wife and her lawyer. The judge, having gotten the full picture from our client, was less intrigued by the wife's testimony. Every now and then he would make some acknowledgment that there was a trial going on, but for the most part he seemed more interested in the newspaper in front of him. Our lawyer kept his mouth shut. There were a couple of times when he might have interrupted with objections, but he let them go unchallenged; he didn't want to re-engage the judge in the wife's testimony.

The other lawyer, meanwhile, was getting more and more frustrated. But what could he do? If he asked the judge to please pay attention, he risked getting told off. He might even be held in contempt, and for sure he would never get a break from that judge in any future cases. Finally, however, as politely as possible, the opposing attorney cleared his throat and said, "Uh, excuse me, Judge?"

"Yes?" the judge growled, not even looking up.

"Uh, Your Honor, if it pleases the court, I just wanted to make sure that my client is speaking loudly and clearly enough, so that the court can hear her. I can instruct her to speak more loudly and clearly . . ."

At that point the judge did look up, sharply. He stared at the attorney and said, slowly, "I think I've heard everything I need to hear. Please continue." And he put his head back down. The lawyer, shaken, did the only thing he could do. He finished the direct examination of his client, and called his other witnesses. Our lawyer continued to stay glued to his seat, silent. Things were going his way, so he wanted to wrap up the trial as soon as possible. The wife's attorney finally ended their side of the case, and the two lawyers made their closing statements. Our lawyer's closing statement was the briefest in a long and successful career. The judge put the paper aside, and then ruled that our client would get everything he asked for.

That's an extreme example, of course. Most judges strive to be fair or at least give the impression of being fair. It's worth noting that most states provide for judges only to hear divorce cases. Even in states such as Texas and Georgia, where it is possible to demand a jury for a divorce trial, it is relatively rare. However, if you're contemplating getting divorced in either of those states, it's even more important to file your divorce petition first so that you can present your case first in the courtroom. We've talked about how judges, even after all their legal training and experience, are still prone to give a lot of weight to the story they hear first, and then look to the other side to respond. Imagine how it is for a jury, a group of people who aren't trained in the law. For the vast majority of jurors, the closest they've come to deciding disputes is literally when their kids have come to them saying, "He hit me!" "She hit me first!" "No, I didn't . . ."

> *Judges, even after all their legal training and experience, are still prone to give a lot of weight to the story they hear first.*

Economic considerations are also a factor in when and whether to file for divorce. It's well known that money troubles are a common reason for couples to divorce. He blames her for spending too much (or vice versa), she blames him for not earning enough (or vice versa), and neither of them likes what the other spends on. As a result, it would make sense for there to be more divorces during economic hard times. But it's not true. Many people are actually less likely to divorce during hard times. For example, the statistics are still coming in for the recession that began in 2008, but many jurisdictions across the country are reporting fewer divorces, not more. Why? Because divorce is expensive. (Which reminds me of the old joke: Why is divorce so expensive? Because it's worth it.)

During tough times, many middle-class and working couples can't afford to hire qualified lawyers. They can't afford to support two households instead of one. So they suck it up and tough it out. They tolerate each other simply because their lifestyles and quality of life would be so much worse if they split up. In such situations it is imperative to resist the urge to agree to an inexpensive or "agreed" divorce that can cost you more later.

But there are reasons that wealthier people avoid divorce during tough times too. Think about it. Wives are more likely to file for divorce than husbands. Wives are more likely to get financial support from husbands than the other way around. Husbands typically make more money during good times than bad times. So when does it make sense for a wife to sue her rich husband for divorce? When he's flush.

That's why we advise men who are considering a divorce to go ahead and file first if they are going through tough times—if they aren't getting any overtime this year, if the usual bonus didn't come through, if they own a business and revenue is down. It's another example of choosing the time and place for battle. If you allow your opponent to choose the time and place, you can be sure she'll choose when she is in the strongest position to ask for more money, and you're in the weakest position to deny her. If you know your marriage is heading toward the rocks, consider whether your wife might simply be waiting for your income and assets to rebound.

Many of our clients are small businessmen, everything from men who run one-man plumbing-repair operations to doctors and other professionals who have a few employees. When they get involved in a divorce, whether they file first or not, the key issue is usually the value of the business. The more it's worth, the more the wife is going to get in every aspect of the financial settlement—dividing up the assets, the monthly maintenance payments, even the child support. And how is the business valued? The single most important factor is the recent revenue. If revenue is down, the value of the business is down, and the man's income is down.

> *It seems odd, but when you're broke and think you can't afford it, that's probably the best time to stand in front of a judge asking for a divorce.*

It seems odd, but when you're broke and think you can't afford it, that's probably the best time to stand in front of a judge asking for a divorce. The judge, by law, has to consider your ability to pay. If you're not making as much money, and if your income has dropped, you don't have as much ability to pay.

The majority of men who come to us for initial consultations do not want to get divorced. Typically, they come in and they're distraught because they've just found out their marriage may be on the rocks.

"Let me guess," I say. "She said you were controlling. She said you don't listen to her. She told you you didn't know her anymore and she didn't know you anymore. She told you she was so unhappy that she wanted a divorce."

The man is now looking at me with a stunned look on his face. It's as if I had eavesdropped on the conversation.

"What you could have done," I continue, "is say, I hear you, honey. I want to try to understand you, and I want to understand what has happened to us. I want to be with you. I want us to be happy. I'll do whatever you want. What do you want me to do? What can I do right now?"

By then the man is frowning. No, that is definitely not how he responded.

"Instead," I go on, "you probably said, hey, what are you talking about? This is stupid. This is crazy talk. You're confused. You don't know what you want . . ."

The man is reluctantly nodding, a look of chagrin on his face. Yeah, that's what he said. I tell him that his response reinforced his wife's perceptions that he was trying to control her and control the marriage. The question then becomes whether there is anything he can do to save the marriage, and whether he is willing to do it.

We don't ever want to take anyone into a divorce if there is a chance of salvaging the marriage. We will never talk anyone into filing. That's not our job—to tell men whether they should be married or not. In fact, every lawyer in our firm has stories about helping couples stay together. "Are you sure there has to be a divorce?" we ask. "Can the marriage be saved? Is there any way? Have you talked to your clergyman? Can we help you arrange to set up counseling?" Our clients need to tell us they want to be divorced. They need to convince us that they are mentally and emotionally prepared to go through with it. They need to convince us that they simply can't live within the marriage anymore. And then our job is to lay out the options and give them the best advice for achieving the best result. We lay out the possible consequences of doing nothing, and we lay out the options and possible results in going forward.

Even if it becomes apparent that a divorce is going to happen, most men simply don't want to be the one to file the papers. As lawyers, my colleagues and I have to tell them the advantages. Sometimes men don't want to file for religious reasons. The Roman Catholic Church, for example, still does not recognize divorce. So sometimes, usually for devout Catholics who don't want to go against the tenets of the church, we will arrange a legal separation instead of a divorce. Yes, in theory they could get an annulment from the Church, but as you might imagine, that can be quite an involved process. It's still easier to go to the local courthouse than to the Vatican for your legal work.

Besides religious reasons, the most common reason for arranging a legal separation instead of a divorce is that the couple wants to keep health insurance or benefits. In that case, we are usually able to arrange all the usual aspects of divorce, but they remain legally married, and thereby keep the health coverage for both of them and the kids, too.

Incidentally, many people mistakenly think that a legal separation is common, and that it is a routine first step toward getting a divorce. Not true. A legal separation is just like a divorce without formally ending the marriage. The property is divided, custody is arranged, maintenance payments are scheduled, and so on. If a couple has a legal separation, there may be no need to go through the entire process again and get a divorce—unless they want to remarry.

There are also many nonreligious reasons that many men

legal separation

don't want to file first. "I don't want people to think I wanted out of the marriage," they say. "I don't want people to think it was my fault." Well, here's a news flash. In our society, no matter who files first, many people—at least initially—are going to assume it was the man's fault. It's a funny thing, though—people soon forget. Within three years most family and friends don't remember who filed first, and most of the time they don't recall why, either. Whether or not anyone thinks he or she was at fault, or that the other one was at fault, perhaps the healthiest attitude is that it was both partners' fault. And in our experience, that is usually the case. An even better attitude, we think, is for the ex-couple to agree, "Hey, no one was at fault. The marriage failed. That's all. We weren't right for each other."

Another reason many men don't want to file first is because of their kids. "I don't want them to think I was the one who ended it," they fret. But that should not be an issue for the kids, especially when they're little. They don't need to know who filed. They shouldn't be part of that discussion, and many couples—even people who feel they have been aggrieved by the other—do a pretty good job of protecting their soon-to-be-ex in the eyes of the kids. They're mature enough to recognize that a healthy relationship with both parents is important to the kids during and after a divorce. Later, when the kids are older, if the issue of who filed first has to be discussed, they will be better able to understand. Conversely, if your wife is out to make you the villain, she's going to try to do that no matter who filed first.

DON'T MAKE A STUPID MISTAKE: CONSIDER FILING FIRST.

CONCEALING INFORMATION FROM YOUR LAWYER

WE DON'T KNOW exactly what happened to Bernie after we handled his case, but he's one of our firm's favorite clients of all time—for the wrong reasons. We talk about Bernie all the time, telling clients about him and what can happen if they do what Bernie did. Let me tell you the story.

Bernie came to us and asked one of my colleagues to represent him in his divorce. He and his soon-to-be-ex both wanted custody of their two kids, a 16-year-old boy and a 12-year-old girl. Since they had split up, the girl had been living with her mom, and the boy had been living with Bernie. Both kids wanted to stay where they were, but each of them wanted to be able to see the other parent occasionally. The only people in the family who didn't get along were Bernie and his wife, and they each wanted custody of both kids.

"I could live with her having permanent custody of my

little girl, but I really want custody of my son," Bernie told my colleague.

Bernie, who worked as the maintenance supervisor for a good-sized apartment complex, seemed like a decent dad, so we told him he had a good chance of getting custody of his son. It didn't look like his soon-to-be-ex was going to agree to an out-of-court settlement, so we prepared for trial. Bernie's case got a big boost when the court appointed a guardian *ad litem* (GAL) for the children. The GAL is usually a lawyer and serves as an independent advocate for the children. The GAL is appointed to do a social study of the family, looking at both the mom and the dad and making recommendations about custody. Judges give these recommendations a lot of weight, and often follow them down to the letter. In Bernie's case, the GAL recommended that the wife get custody of the girl and that Bernie get custody of the boy. "That's good news," my colleague told Bernie. "I know that this judge, who is very fair, typically follows the GAL's recommendations."

But we still had to go to trial, and anything can happen at trial. The case proceeded routinely right up until we were almost finished. The wife testified first, then Bernie, and then the guardian *ad litem* testified and made the recommendation that Bernie get the boy and the wife get the girl. My colleague was extremely confident; Bernie's case seemed like it was in the bag.

Then came a surprise. After the initial testimony of both parties and the GAL, each party has an option for rebuttal testimony—an opportunity for a lawyer to call a witness to knock down the other party's testimony. In this case, the wife's lawyer called her back to the stand.

"Did you ever see your husband dealing drugs?" the lawyer asked.

My colleague was shocked. Bernie had never mentioned dealing drugs in their discussions about possible negative history that would affect the custody case. This was the first time it had come up in the case. My colleague turned to Bernie, but he was staring at his hands on the table in front of him.

"Yes," the wife said. "Many times."

Under further questioning from her attorney, the wife testified that her father was a longtime marijuana dealer, and that he and Bernie had formed a partnership. Bernie sold drugs to residents of the apartment complex where he worked.

The judge was not happy. "In my chambers," he directed the lawyers.

Behind closed doors, the judge addressed my colleague. "Your client has a tough choice," the judge told her. "He gets on the stand and waives his Fifth Amendment right to self-incrimination or he lets this allegation go unrebutted."

Bernie reluctantly agreed to testify—and risk criminal charges—because otherwise he would give up any chance of custody. Bernie said he had stopped dealing drugs a year earlier, when the divorce was filed. My colleague was skeptical. "Before you get up there," she said, "I need you to finally tell me the truth. Can you pass a drug test right now?"

"Um, uh, I don't think so," Bernie said. He claimed he had also quit smoking pot when the divorce proceedings began. But he said he had fired up a bowl the night before the trial. "A lot of stress," he said.

My colleague's experience with dozens of cases involving substance abuse told her that he had probably been smoking pot all along. No wonder the 16-year-old boy wanted to live with him.

Bernie took the stand, and it was obvious that the judge thought he was lying. The judge gave both kids to the mom.

Afterward, Bernie didn't have much of an explanation for why he withheld such important information. "I didn't think she'd bring it up because of her dad," he explained lamely.

Looking back, if Bernie had come clean with my colleague, he may well have ended up winning custody of his son. That's the point we try to make when we tell this story over and over to prospective clients. That's why Bernie is a favorite client—he's become a symbol for one of the biggest knucklehead things a man can do in a divorce: keep information from his lawyer. Bernie simply assumed—hoped, actually—that his wife would never mention his drug dealing.

If Bernie had told my colleague everything at the start of the case, she would have told him to stop dealing and stop using drugs. That might actually have worked in Bernie's favor: He was a pot user and dealer when he was living with his wife, because she was such a bad influence, and her father was the one who led him into becoming a dealer. The wife's father might have been deposed to push the issue at the front end of the case, not a case-concluding bombshell. My colleague could have argued that once Bernie was free of his wife and her father's bad influence, he was straight and clean and a much better parent—a much better parent than the wife, who was still in close contact with her father. My colleague could have made her complicit in the drug dealing, right alongside Bernie. Instead, in court she came across as the whistle-blower while he came across as the bad guy.

"When you keep something from your attorney," we warn clients, "it's like trying to build a house on a fault line in the earth. At some point there

> *When you keep something from your attorney, it's like trying to build a house on a fault line in the earth. At some point there is going to be an earthquake, and it's all going to come tumbling down.*

is going to be an earthquake, and it's all going to come tumbling down."

Lawyers routinely urge clients to tell them everything, whether it's common knowledge or a closely guarded secret. Of course, we don't really mean *everything*. We mean everything that might be important. Just because it is common knowledge or even public record (bankruptcy, lawsuits, criminal charges, or published incidents), don't assume your lawyer knows about it or that the other side will point it out. Don't be ashamed, don't be embarrassed. We've probably heard it before. And whether we've heard it before or not, we're not going to go around telling anyone. By law, whatever is discussed in confidence with your lawyer will remain confidential. Disclosing such confidences would be unethical under the attorney-client privilege. We're not going to bring it up, but we want to be prepared.

If it's a potentially criminal issue, I need to know that. Examples include skimming money from business accounts at work, cheating on taxes, collecting on false insurance claims, and bankruptcy fraud. Often the wife either already knows or is involved herself. If the wife's attorney asks about it, even during a pretrial deposition, the client has to either admit to a crime or lie about it and commit perjury, which just adds one more crime to the list. If a lawyer knows about criminal behavior first, the lawyer can help the client deal with it and prepare for the questions under oath. People really do sometimes plead the Fifth Amendment, refusing to answer on the constitutional grounds that it may incriminate them. It's not just on TV; it happens in real life too.

THE WHOLE TRUTH

We tell our clients that the most valuable thing they have in their case is their credibility—their credibility with their lawyer, with their children, with social workers or the guardian *ad litem*, and especially with the judge. "The moment your credibility is called into question, even slightly, is the moment you start to lose ground in your case," we warn. "The judge has only a very short period of time to get to know you and form an impression of you. If the judge hears one inconsistency or one lie or untruth, it colors everything else you have to say."

Of course, sometimes a client might honestly forget about a tiny 401(k) from three jobs and fifteen years ago, or about a small piece of property in the woods that his great-aunt left him twenty years ago. But don't try to tell your lawyer—or a judge—that you forgot about that offshore bank account you set up two years ago or about your part-time job as a carpenter. And even if it's an honest mistake, it makes you look bad if the other side's lawyer brings up something you have not mentioned, even a small 401(k) or your interest in a long-forgotten piece of land. If your wife knows about it, she probably told her lawyer. At trial is not the time to find out that she paid better attention to your financial affairs than you thought she did.

Some clients don't provide any information at all. Two types of men seem to fall into this category. One type doesn't want a divorce. We tell them what we need, over and over, but they simply don't give it to us. They think that if they don't hand over that bank statement or don't produce those tax records, maybe this whole nightmare will go away. They're in denial, and thereby denying their attorney time to review the information and plan the case. Further, they are only delaying the inevitable; opposing counsel will obtain the information by subpoena eventually.

The other men who drag their feet on providing information are the high-flyers, often professionals or executives. Maybe they don't like the idea of someone telling them what to do when we insist, "Get those records for me." Maybe they think it's beneath them, that it's something that an administrative assistant should handle. Well, we don't care. Have an administrative assistant handle it. Just get it to us. If you say you can't find your bank records, we can contact the bank and get them for you, but it is going to cost time and money, and add significantly to your legal fees. (Most lawyers, at least at our firm, really do work hard to keep fees down. We profit more by keeping fees down and getting more referrals than by running up avoidable costs.)

I've had men try to hide their gambling problems, or "forget" to mention that little detail about a DWI arrest. Inevitably, those things come back to bite us—and surprise us, to make matters worse—at a trial. If your wife knows something about you, then you'd better assume her lawyer is going to know it too. And if your wife and her lawyer know something about you, they might use it against you. If you once threw a shoe at your wife, I want to know about it—even if you missed her on purpose—because she might cite that as an example of your violent tendencies. If you once said, "I wish I was dead," I want to know, because she could claim you are suicidal. If you once stuck a few free samples of Claritin in your pocket in the examining room when your doctor's back was turned, I want to know, because she might cite it as an example of your dishonesty or your reliance on drugs. You might think those are ridiculous examples, but they're not.

Your lawyer needs to know anything and everything your wife might say about you to hurt you or your case.

Your lawyer needs to know anything and everything your wife might say about you to hurt you or your case.

Even if you are sure it's something your wife doesn't know about, tell us anyway. I once had a client who was absolutely sure his wife did not know about a bank account he kept secretly on the side. He had used the money in the account to fund a number of affairs over the years, paying for dinners, drinks, and hotel rooms with his girlfriends. If the client had told me about the bank account, we would have had to include it in the financial statements, and his soon-to-be-ex-wife would have been entitled to half of the money in the account—plus it would have been proof of his philandering. But the client didn't tell me. He figured there was no way his wife could know about it. But she did. One of his ex-girlfriends was angry with him for dumping her, and she told the wife about the account. The wife's lawyer sprung it on us in court. As often happens when a judge finds out that a man is trying to hide assets, the judge awarded the entire amount in the account to the wife.

Some men think that if they can hide an asset until the divorce decree becomes final, they're in the clear. Not so. I had a client who sold a lot of stock when he realized a divorce was on the horizon. He sprinkled the proceeds into a bunch of bank accounts here and there. He disclosed a couple of the accounts, but not all. His wife's lawyer hired financial consultants—that's not unusual in cases involving a lot of money or complicated holdings—to go through the books. The consultants found almost everything—all but a couple of offshore accounts that had a combined total of about $100,000. I asked the client if what the wife's consultants found was everything and he said yes. The two sides reached a settlement that was approved by the court, and the case was closed. The client figured he had saved himself about $50,000, since his wife hadn't found the $100,000 in offshore accounts and avoided having to give her half.

About six months later, a statement from an offshore investment house came to the client's former home address, where his ex-wife still lived. Puzzled, she handed it to her lawyer. Her lawyer handed it to the financial consultants, who quickly tracked down the account. My client was busted. He came dragging back to me crying for help, but there was nothing I could do. He had lied to his wife, to the financial consultants, to the court, and to me, his lawyer. The ex-wife's lawyer petitioned the court and the case was reopened. The settlement decree was altered and my former client was ordered to give his ex-wife an additional $100,000 plus her attorney fees in reopening the case. Why lie, and risk losing not only your self-respect but twice as much as it would cost you to tell the truth?

Another client, Drew, was retired, in his early sixties. His children were grown and gone, but his wife wanted more financial support than he thought he could pay. "All I have to live on is my retirement benefit," he told us. "I don't have any other income." Okay, we said. We helped Drew work out a budget that showed him spending every nickel of his monthly pension on a pretty frugal lifestyle. The only thing that might have been considered extravagant was that he had one of those special NFL television packages that let you see every game every Sunday. He was a football nut, and to him the extra $59.99 a month was a necessity.

At the same time, his wife insisted that he had been supporting her, and she couldn't live without a fair chunk of whatever he had contributed to the household. So with no settlement, we went to trial. When our client got on the stand, our lawyer walked him through his finances, exactly the way we had laid them out in evidence. Then the wife's attorney stood up to cross-examine our client.

After some introductory pleasantries, he asked, "Sir, where exactly were you last Thursday afternoon?" Our attorney was puzzled. What was this about? Who cared where he was last Thursday?

"Uh, I'm not exactly sure," our client replied.

"Perhaps I can help you remember," the lawyer said. "Were you at the site of a home renovation going on at 111 Crest Avenue?"

"I might have been," our client said. "I guess I was."

I won't lay out the rest of the excruciating testimony, but it turns out our client was working about half-time on a building site, doing carpentry work. It further turned out, under more questioning, that he often worked handyman jobs around town, picking up $12 or sometimes $15 an hour. Our client professed not to know how much he made, but finally admitted that it was sometimes up to $400 a week. Yes, he conceded, he brought in $12,000 to $15,000 during the previous year.

Of course, the judge hammered the carpenter. He not only was ordered to pay his ex-wife part of his retirement benefits, but he also was ordered to pay her $500 a month.

"Tell me the worst thing she could possibly say about you," I tell clients. "Whether it's true or not."

If you hit your wife, I want to hear about it. "I'm not judging you," I tell my clients. "I don't care what you tell me. The point is I need to know it so I can be prepared for it if you're sitting on the stand or in a deposition. If I know, I can prepare and defend you. The facts are what they are. We have to deal with them. I want to be ready. And I don't want you lying under oath."

Speaking of perjury, clients do ask us about that. Sometimes they have done something wrong, and they want to know if it's all right to shade the truth while under oath. I think they expect us to wink at them, or give them some sort of signal that it's okay because this happens all the time in court. Well, we're not going to do that. We're not going to encourage or endorse or in any way approve any sort of testimony that is not accurate. Under oath, in response to questioning from your wife's attorney, you can answer the questions as narrowly and precisely as possible. But you must tell "nothing but the truth."

We were recently involved in a case where the wife was independently wealthy, an heiress, and she was asked questions specifically about her trust fund. The heiress answered artfully. She made it sound as if the trust fund was her sole source of income, about $500,000 a year. When it eventually came out on cross-examination that the heiress actually had two other trust funds paying her more than $1 million a year, she ended up paying through the nose, and her attorney ended up on the wrong end of an ethics investigation.

In another case, one of our lawyers was blindsided when the wife testified that her husband once tried to kill himself. Our lawyer was able to get a quick recess and ask our client: "What? You tried to kill yourself?" No, the client said. He had gotten hurt at work—he had an awkward fall and broke his shoulder—and he had been given some very strong painkillers. The pills made him dopey but didn't seem to dull the pain. He had simply forgotten that he had taken some, and then he took some more, and then he did it again. His wife came home, found him unconscious, and called 911. He was taken to the hospital, but he was okay. He didn't even have his stomach pumped. He apologized for not telling his lawyer about it, but it hadn't seemed important to him. Until that moment at the trial, no one—not even his doctors—had raised the question about whether he was suicidal. Our lawyer was able to cross-examine the wife, who had no medical or psychological documentation to support her surprise testimony, and discredit her.

In contrast, a client named Al told one of our lawyers right up front, at their very first meeting, that he had been treated for mental illness. The documents from his wife said that since he had guns in his house she was afraid of what might happen if he got really angry and she wasn't there to calm him down and protect the kids, two boys aged nine and five. She was so afraid that he was unstable, and that he would hurt himself or the kids, that she wanted full custody of the kids. For his own good, she said. Al had told his lawyer, my colleague, about the guns, too, so that wasn't a surprise, either.

So my colleague was able to prepare. He suggested that while the divorce was pending, Al have a social worker supervise his visits with the kids to provide an objective observer to counter his wife's claims. The social worker could gauge his stability, and also look around and make sure the guns were safely stored. The court agreed, much to the mother's dismay. She hadn't wanted Al to see his kids at all. She wanted to take them away from him completely. But the court agreed with us and approved a schedule of supervised visits. Al did well during the visits, and so did the kids. The social worker said he had not exhibited any anger issues when things did not go as planned. He seemed to have a good relationship with the kids, and the guns were not an issue. When it came to trial—the wife would not settle unless she got full custody—the social worker testified, "I don't have any concerns about his stability or his parenting abilities."

Al himself took the stand and said, "I understand why there are concerns about my mental health. I appreciate my wife's concern for our children. But with the help of doctors and medication, I am feeling like my old self again. I haven't missed any days of work, I am exercising regularly, I am going to church, and my doctors are reducing the strength and the frequency of my medication. I would like to get off the medication completely, if my psychiatrist approves. No matter what, I intend to continue seeing a therapist." Al made sense, and the judge went along with our request for a shared-custody plan—unsupervised—that let him have the kids on alternate weekends and half of the big holidays each year.

Lawyers are always concerned about whether a client is hiding something in his past, but it can be even worse when a client refuses to tell the lawyer something new that has come up, something that happened just yesterday. I had a client who had some alcohol issues. He knew it was going to be part of the case. His wife had been bugging him about his drinking for years, and finally threw him out of the house and demanded a divorce. So he did the right thing and told us about it up front. In truth, our lawyers didn't think his problems were all that bad. He was a factory worker, and there was no record of his missing work because of drinking. He had no police record, and nobody was claiming that he had ever hit his wife or their three kids. The only big thing we could find was that once he went with one of the kids on a campout and got drunk on some whiskey one of the other dads had smuggled along. He was dancing around the campfire and generally acting like a drunken fool, but that wasn't until after the kids had retired to their tents and gone to sleep. None of the kids saw it, including our client's own son. The other dads poured our client into a sleeping bag, he had a bad headache on the hike the next day, and that was the end of it. One of the other dads' wives told our client's wife about it a week later. So yeah, our client looked bad. But in the realm of drunken escapades we've encountered as divorce lawyers, that's barely a 2 on a 10-point scale.

His wife, however, was really upset about the drinking, and her lawyer was pushing the issue hard in terms of custody. They wanted to severely limit his time with their kids, to a single hour a week, and that had to be supervised, during the day, and at a clinic or church. The implication was that he would show up drunk, or get drunk while with the kids.

We thought that was too severe, and it seemed like the court was going to agree with us when we went to a hearing for temporary orders to determine custody. But the wife's attorney held up a clipping from the "Police Blotter" section of the most recent edition of the weekly newspaper in the small town where they lived. The brief little article, one short paragraph, noted that our client had been arrested for driving under the influence five days earlier. Our client hadn't told us. It was game over. If we had known about the arrest and been able to spin it even a little bit, our client might have ended up with a better custody arrangement. Maybe our attorney could have sat down with the other attorney and worked out a settlement before they found out about the DWI. But it was too late. Our client was granted only one hour of supervised visitation a week. It was so disheartening to our client, so difficult to see his kids under those circumstances, that he stopped going to the visitations. The last we heard, after the divorce he drifted away from his kids and never saw them.

On the other hand, we had a recent case that was about to go to trial—the couple were far apart on both money and custody—when our client called us on a Monday morning and said he had been arrested for DWI over the weekend. The police report confirmed that there was no one else in his car, no accident or injury, and his blood alcohol level was just over the legal limit. Not excusable, but it was his first DWI and our client was otherwise an upstanding father. Our lawyer swung into action, immediately calling the other side's attorney and suggesting they meet for a settlement conference before they could find out about the DWI. We offered more money than we had been offering and asked for less custody. The wife's lawyer took the new offer back to her, and she took the settlement rather than go through the hassle of a trial. If she known about the DWI, she might have used it at trial and our client might have ended with a much worse deal.

Your lawyer wants to know everything about you, but your lawyer wants to know everything about your soon-to-be-ex too. This is no time for gallantry, or to be embarrassed that you tolerated her shortcomings. This is the time to dish. Here's a recent example. Joe came to us heartbroken. He was only 24, his wife was only 22, and they had been married less than two years. But she had a boyfriend and wanted a divorce. Joe was a security guard, a nice guy, and didn't have a lot of money, but the young wife—who had not worked since they got married—wanted most of it. Our position was that they were young, they had been married just a short time, they had no significant joint assets, and they had no kids—so they should just split their meager savings and checking accounts down the middle, divide up the IKEA furniture they had bought together, and each keep the CDs, electronics, and cars they had brought to the marriage. He shouldn't have to support her just because she wasn't working; in most states, women who aren't caring for children at home are presumed to be able to go out and work. But the wife wouldn't hear of it. She wanted some of Joe's earnings as a security guard.

Our lawyer was in the hallway outside the courtroom for the hearing for temporary orders when Joe arrived, looking flushed.

"I don't know if I should tell you this," Joe began. It seemed like he was going to cry. He composed himself and continued. "I think my wife is pregnant. I don't think the baby is mine. I think it's her boyfriend's."

Talk about a bombshell. "What do we do?" Joe asked. My colleague asked Joe a few questions, and between the two of them they figured out that the baby would be born in late summer or early autumn. But the divorce probably wouldn't be finalized until after that, later in the autumn.

"We have to tell the judge," my colleague said. "We've got to get this out there, on the table. Otherwise the baby will be born while the divorce is pending, while you're still married. All she has to do is say you're the father, and since you're still married, you're presumed to be the father. We can fight that presumption, but that can be a lot of time, trouble, and expense. We've got to make sure the judge knows right away that she's pregnant, and that you don't think the baby is yours."

My colleague and our client went into the courtroom and took their seats at the table on their side. The judge wanted to see the two attorneys in chambers, without the clients, which is not unusual in hearings. The judge simply wants to get the lay of the land and understand what is happening, and an informal conversation in private, in the judge's office behind the courtroom, often makes things go more smoothly in open court.

"So," the judge said to the two attorneys. "What have we got here?"

The wife's attorney outlined what the wife was looking for: money. The judge nodded and looked at my colleague. What did Joe want?

"Before we get into any specifics, Your Honor," our lawyer said, "it has come to my attention that the wife may be pregnant, and that it is very likely that her husband is not the father."

The judge looked surprised and the wife's attorney looked shocked. "Excuse me, please, for a moment," she said. "I need to speak with my client." She went back to the courtroom, huddled with the wife for a couple of minutes, and came back wearing a very stern face, sort of a combination of anger and embarrassment. "It's true," the lawyer said. "She's pregnant, and she was afraid to tell me. She's not sure who the father is. I guess we'll need to have tests done."

The tests subsequently showed that Joe was not the father, so the issue of him paying child support never came up. The rest of the case disappeared, too, since they lived in a state that considered marital misconduct when determining alimony. Obviously, the wife should have told her lawyer she was pregnant. I don't know if her lawyer could have done anything differently, but it probably would have avoided the embarrassment, credibility, and waste of court time to address her claim for support from her husband.

As a client, you have to overcome the part of human nature that colors your memories and your interpretations. We all try to put ourselves in a good light. We play down the stupid things we do, and rationalize them. We reinterpret events, and our motives, and what we may have been thinking at the time. It's human nature to do that. When you're talking to your lawyer, don't try to spin information. Try to see things

When you're talking to your lawyer, don't try to spin information.

from your wife's point of view, rather than your own. Think of the client with the work injury who accidentally overmedicated himself with painkillers. To his wife, years later, it was a suicide attempt. We all have different interpretations. That's normal. Try to give your lawyer every possible interpretation, especially the worst one. Don't try to make yourself look good.

We see this a lot with domestic violence. Imagine the parallel conversations going on between a husband and his attorney, and a wife and her attorney. The two attorneys are asking basically the same questions, but the husband and wife have entirely different takes on what happened. Imagine a split screen, the husband talking to his attorney in his office, and across town the wife talking to her attorney in another office.

ATTORNEYS: Any violence issues in the household?
HUSBAND: No, not really.
WIFE: Yes.

ATTORNEYS: Did either of you ever strike each other?
HUSBAND: No.
WIFE: I thought he was going to hit me several times.

ATTORNEYS: Were the police ever involved?
HUSBAND: My wife called them once, but it was just during an argument and she was upset. We talked to them and they left. No charges.
WIFE: I thought he was going to hit me, so I called 911. The police took him outside and calmed him down and told him if he ever touched me or I called again that they would take him to jail.

See the differences in the two sets of answers? The similarities? The husband and wife are talking about the same scenario, but each has an entirely different spin. Is either one inaccurate? Technically, no. From their respective points of view, that is what happened. But the mere fact that the wife is giving more detail probably gives her version more weight. The husband is reciting the facts, but maybe not all the facts.

If I know only his version of what happened when the cops came, I've got one hand tied behind my back. If I know she's going to say she thought he was going to hit her, and she called 911, and the cops took him outside to cool him off, well, I can do something about that. I can prepare for her version. I can question him more, and explain why he was angry with her in the first place—she was waving a knife at him. If it seemed like he was going to hit her, that was purely out of self-defense. Maybe she had been threatening to call 911 for a long time, including whenever he raised a topic she didn't want to talk about, like running up big credit card bills and hiding them. Maybe I interview the cops and see what they remember of the incident; maybe they don't remember it all, which is good for our side. I can put the discussion outside with the cops in the context of being advice to seek counsel from a lawyer about getting a divorce, and maybe a restraining order against her. There are always possibilities, but if I don't know the whole story then I don't know the possibilities.

THE TRUTH CUTS BOTH WAYS

Don't try to gloss things over. If it's something that might be important, tell us. We'll decide whether it is important to your case. Here's a great example of a client getting priorities mixed up. Rocco and his wife loved living a rural, outdoorsy lifestyle. They just didn't like living it together. Part of the problem apparently was that Rocco had become something of a health nut. They lived on several acres out in the country, and he became a vegetarian and devoted a lot of time to growing organic vegetables and trying to get their seven-year-old daughter to be a vegetarian, too. Rocco's wife thought this was crazy, and as their relationship fell apart she tormented him by bringing home cheeseburgers and fries. She not only ate them in front of him, but gave them to the little girl. The kid, of course, loved going to McDonald's, and that drove Rocco crazy. When they finally agreed to divorce, there was a custody battle, and he wanted us to paint his wife as a bad parent for feeding the kid fast food. "It's poison," he said.

We were not sure how far we'd get under the theory that a parent should be denied custody for giving the kid a burger and fries once a week. We kept asking Rocco, hey, what else have you got? It was hard to get him to focus on anything else. Finally we sat him down and had him tell us about a recent weekend. Yes, his wife had taken the kid out to Burger King. Yes, we understood that he believed that fast food was ruining his daughter's life. But what else did they do that weekend? Well, Rocco told us, he had taken the truck to the hardware store, and he had wanted his daughter to come along with him, but his wife instead talked her into going for a motorcycle ride.

Wait a minute, our lawyer said. A motorcycle ride? Your wife has a motorcycle? She takes the seven-year-old on the back of a motorcycle? Where? When? How often?

It took a while, but it emerged that the mom often took the kid on her dirt bike on paths on their property, and on short trips on local roads, like to the Burger King. Fortunately, our lawyer asked the $64,000 question: What kind of helmet does the little girl wear?

Rocco shrugged, unconcerned. "Oh, she doesn't wear a helmet," he said. Bingo. Mom took her daughter on the back of a motorcycle without a helmet. That example of risky and reckless behavior gave us the leverage we needed to open the door to a discussion about the mother's judgment and how good a parent she was. That ended up carrying a lot more weight in the case than fast food as poison. Rocco went from looking like he would have to scramble to see his daughter once a week to winning 50-50 joint custody. And the judge ordered the mother to buy the girl a helmet and make her wear it.

Men misjudge the importance not only of things their wives do, but also things they have done themselves. And sometimes their attorneys give them good advice about some past indiscre-

Men misjudge the importance not only of things their wives do, but also things they have done themselves.

tion, and they ignore it. Here's a stark example. We had a recent case in a small town in a conservative area in the Midwest. Our client's name was Ralph, and he ran a sporting goods store. He and his wife were splitting up because she had a boyfriend, and he wanted custody of their nine-year-old daughter. The attorney in our firm who handled the case thought Ralph had a pretty good chance at winning 50-50 joint custody, at least, and maybe more. The mom wasn't a bad parent, but Ralph seemed to be a better parent. He was the one who took the girl to her doctor's appointments, went to parent-teacher conferences, drove her to playdates and piano lessons, and once a month took her to the nearest big city, about two hours away, to go to a museum or a concert or do some other cultural activity. On paper, Ralph was a great parent. His wife had instigated the breakup and moved out of their home several months earlier, leaving Ralph as his daughter's primary caregiver, so that was in Ralph's favor, too. On top of it all, the girl was doing better—academically, socially, in every way—since her mom had moved out.

In talking to us, Ralph's only worry was that he had started dating recently. He had met a woman, and they were spending a lot of time together. That seemed to be fine with his daughter, but he worried that his soon-to-be-ex could use that against him in the divorce proceedings. "Don't worry," my colleague told Ralph. "It's no big deal, she's got a boyfriend, you've got a girlfriend, everybody is moving on, everything is normal."

Except everything was not normal, and our lawyer did not find out how abnormal until the hearing for temporary orders. Ralph was seeking primary custody and his wife, even though she had moved out, wanted a 50-50 arrangement. It emerged that Ralph and his new girlfriend had been taking showers together—with the nine-year-old daughter. The judge granted temporary joint custody—provided Ralph stop including the little girl in the group showers. Our attorney was very upset that everyone else knew about this—including Ralph's wife and her attorney—but Ralph had not mentioned it to his own attorney.

"What's the big deal?" he asked our attorney later. "The human body is beautiful. I'm trying to help my daughter get over the hang-ups so many of us have over our bodies. This helps her develop very positive attitudes toward her own body, and toward the body in general." He showed our lawyer an article from a Swedish magazine advocating gang showers for families—and for friends, if more than one family happens to, say, go camping together.

"Ralph," our lawyer said. "In this part of the world, people in general—and judges in particular—are not necessarily as modern and progressive as those people taking showers together with the kids in Sweden. Around here, that is strange."

Our lawyer told Ralph he really had to cut it out. "It doesn't appear that it has affected your daughter," our lawyer said, "but you've got to knock it off. If you stop now, and your wife's lawyer brings it up before the judge, we can say it was something you tried because you want to be a good parent, but you realized it was strange, so you stopped, and it's all in the past now. No more group showers." Ralph agreed to stop showering with his girlfriend and his daughter—at least until the divorce decree became final.

Several months later, as the case was about to go to trial, our lawyer was stunned to get a report from a court-appointed psychologist that said Ralph was still taking showers with his daughter. The psychologist said she was considering reporting Ralph to the state social services agency to determine whether the kid should be taken away—and whether Ralph should be reported to the police. Our lawyer telephoned Ralph immediately. Ralph abruptly fired our attorney, right there on the phone.

"I'll represent myself," he said. He ended up getting very limited time with his daughter, which was too bad because otherwise he really was a good parent. If only he had told our lawyer about the showers up front, and then listened to our lawyer's advice, he would probably be a much happier man today. And his kid would probably be better off.

Men often misjudge the importance of one particular fact: cheating wives. As lawyers, we try to be sympathetic and listen. We know it's tough any time someone you love has betrayed you and wants to leave you for someone else. You were good enough for her once, but not anymore. She's found someone better. That used to matter much more, years ago, in divorce law. If one party committed adultery, that party was at fault, and that was cause for divorce. But things have changed. Many states have no-fault divorce, and even states that still ascribe fault tend to downplay infidelity. In truth, in most divorce cases, and especially in terms of dividing the property, the law and the courts don't much care if somebody had an affair as long as the children weren't harmed or marital funds weren't misused.

But some men can't get over it. They want revenge. They need to make it public, they need to punish her, they need to make her suffer. I remember we had one client who simply couldn't let it go. "This is the worst thing she could have done to me," he told us. "Killing me would have been better." He said this made her a horrible person and a horrible parent. He wanted full custody and wanted her to see their kids as little as possible. It took the judge about two minutes to shoot down that whole rationale. Having an affair typically doesn't mean the mom is a bad parent. It means she fell out of love, or she found someone else. It happens, it's human. The law has become less and less interested in the emotional side of divorce and more and more focused solely on the contractual aspects. If that client had been running the case, he probably would have showed himself to be angry and irrational; his wife might have won full custody. Instead, we finally got him to focus a little on other aspects of his wife's life—she mishandled their money, she kept getting fired from jobs, she didn't get along with his parents—and we built on a series of small things to the point where we were able to get the client shared custody.

Sometimes in divorce cases both parties have skeletons that they'd like to keep in the closet, and they tacitly agree not to bring them up. She won't mention that he hit her, and he won't mention that he hit her because she was waving a butcher knife.

I once had a client who told me that he and his soon-to-be-ex had been swingers—they would go to parties where they'd swap partners with other couples and have sex orgies, sometimes with multiple partners over the course of the evening, one after another, and sometimes multiple partners at once, threesomes and foursomes. His soon-to-be-ex told her lawyer, too. They were involved in a custody battle, but everybody reached an unspoken agreement not to mention the wife-swapping—don't ask, don't tell—since both were equally involved. It never came up during the proceedings. I've got to tell you, though, that throughout the proceedings, the soon-to-be-exes often looked at each other with blazing, angry eyes, and then looked away. I wondered if they were thinking, (a) hey, I could destroy him or her if I told about the wife-swapping, and then, (b) oops, I'd be destroying myself, too. It was like a staredown. I, for one, was glad neither of them blinked.

The bottom line is that we know it's impossible for a client to tell his lawyer *everything*. A wife might bring up something the husband said seven years earlier in the heat of an argument, and it hadn't made any difference then or any time since then. But she might bring it up. The important thing is for a man going through divorce to at least hit the highlights of things that might work against him—and then let the lawyer explore the various topics if necessary. If you cheated on your taxes or with another woman, tell your lawyer. If you sometimes holler or sometimes get sullen, tell your lawyer.

**DON'T MAKE A STUPID MISTAKE:
TELL YOUR LAWYER EVERYTHING THAT
MIGHT WORK AGAINST YOU.**

NEGLECTING
THE CHILDREN

REMEMBER THE COUPLE who were swingers? The wife swappers from the previous chapter? Yeah, you remember. There was one other thing about their case that was a little unusual.

The dad, John, was seeking to become the primary residential parent for their two kids, aged 15 and 13. He wanted to let his wife, Kylie, have the kids two nights a week and on alternate weekends. She wanted it the other way around: she wanted residential custody, and he could have the kids one night a week and on alternate weekends.

At the outset, when the client first came to us, it seemed like a toss-up. John was a good parent, but so was Kylie. Apparently the kids never knew about the wife swapping, and it didn't seem to be a factor in family life. Our lawyer thought the client had a decent shot at shared 50-50 joint custody, but probably not residential custody. But then two things happened. First, and most important, John jumped in after the breakup and by sheer force of will became the primary parent. He had always been involved, and he had an advantage because he stayed in the house and Kylie left (we were never sure if it was for someone she met on the swinging circuit). But he did everything he could with and for the kids. He made them their lunches, he drove them to school, he went to the practices and appointments. He was a long-distance trucker, and he juggled his schedule so that he did his driving when his wife had the kids. Whenever Kylie wanted John to keep the kids on her time, he did. He never asked her to take the kids on his time.

Things were going along like that as the divorce was proceeding, and then the other thing happened. Kylie out of the blue decided she wanted to move to another state. She packed the kids up one weekend and took them. It was only the next state over, about 100 miles away, but that's a no-no in the eyes of the courts. She didn't have permission. Our lawyer went to court to obtain an order for her to return with the kids, which she was required to do. That, along with the fact that both kids were saying they didn't want to move to another state and they wanted to live with Dad, made it an easy decision for the judge in the final divorce decree: Our client, John, got residential custody. If Kylie wanted to see the kids in the neighboring state, she could drive over and get them on alternate weekends—as long as they were back at John's on Sunday evening.

A lot of fathers come to us and say, "I want custody." Or they say, "I want the kids as much as possible." They say this, of course, when they first come to us, when the pain is the worst and they are at their lowest. It is our job as lawyers to (a) find out how much they really—I mean really—want custody, and (b) to explain to them just what they have to do to put themselves in position for that to happen.

Dads typically have an uphill battle, no doubt. The old stereotypes and double standards still exist. In our society, moms are widely regarded as the more competent parents. Moms gave birth to the kids. Moms breast-fed them. Moms kissed the kids' boo-boos and made their favorite sandwiches for lunch and bought them their clothes. In many families, the mom is the more involved parent. In most families, at least according to the old stereotypes, the dad is away from home more, working to bring home the bacon. The old stereotype is fading, of course, but it is still deeply imprinted on our culture.

Male clients, we find, often look for logic and linear progress in their divorce cases. They want a fair outcome: fair for the kids, mostly, but also fair for themselves and for their ex-wives. In the court system, however, fairness is more of a goal than a reality. It is often an illusion. The reality is that the old stereotypes survive in the form of double standards. We see it all the time. A couple splits up. They agree to share responsibilities for the kids. Suppose the mom misses one of Junior's baseball games. Well, people say, that's understandable; after all, she's a busy single mom. On the other hand, suppose the dad misses the next game. Well, people say, he's a dad who doesn't care very much about his kids. That is the level of unfairness and illogic we encounter all the time in the world of divorce, and male clients have to face up to it.

It doesn't matter—and it shouldn't matter to you—if your soon-to-be-ex didn't take Junior to his game. If she misses a game, that doesn't mean you get a free pass to miss the next game, when it's your turn to take him. Don't get hung up in thinking that if she lets the kids down, that helps your case. It probably doesn't. But if she lets the kids down and you step up, maybe—just maybe—that will help your case. It's what *you* do that matters. If you find out that your soon-to-be-ex didn't help your daughter with her volcano project or didn't get your son a Halloween costume, jump in there and do it. Drop everything and build a volcano, or make a run to the costume shop. When she falls she falls down on the parenting job, she's a martyr, a victim of divorce. When you fall down on the parenting job, you're a bad dad. So step up whenever and wherever you can. Don't do it because it will help your case. Do it because it's the right thing to do.

> *When she falls down on the parenting job, she's a martyr, a victim of divorce. When you fall down on the parenting job, you're a bad dad. So step up whenever and wherever you can.*

Men may be at a cultural disadvantage in the custody contest. But that doesn't mean men are helpless. If you want custody, you can let your lawyer educate you about the process. You can make a plan. You can never be sure it's going to work, and that you're going to get your kids as much as you want. But if you don't make a plan and carry it out, you can be almost certain that you will not get the custody arrangements you want. You can set a tone of competence and involvement from the very beginning, and you can carry it through the divorce proceedings. Yes, your behavior and involvement before the breakup are significant, but what matters even more is your behavior and involvement from the moment you first meet with your lawyer, set out your priorities, and walk out the door with a plan.

Some judges may seem to be biased toward women. A few may seem biased toward men. A good, experienced lawyer knows which are which, and conducts cases accordingly, including a change of judge if possible. But most judges are open-minded and fair. The reason that women seem to fare better in custody contests is that judges look at most families and see that the mom has been the primary parent while the dad has spent more time away from the house working. The old question—"What's best for the kids?"—carries the most weight. If one parent has stayed home 95 percent of the time, the divorce is probably going to be less of a disruption for the kids if they spend most of their time with that parent—usually the mom.

"But they're my kids, too," the dad says. "I want 50-50 custody."

"Look," the judge in effect says to the dad. "When you and your wife were together, you decided to raise your kids in this manner. Mom would be the primary at-home parent. Taking care of the kids was mainly her responsibility. Working and providing for the family financially was primarily your responsibility. That's how you divided up the duties and how you decided to run your marriage. What's different now? She's still the full-time at-home parent, and you're still the full-time breadwinner."

The number of *Leave It to Beaver* households that we see— the dad off working, the mom home full-time—has dramatically decreased in recent years. In most households the mom works, too, at least part-time. But for better or worse, in many two-parent households the mom neither works as many hours nor earns as much money as her husband. She may not be the 100 percent mom that June Cleaver was and the husband may not be the 100 percent breadwinner that Ward Cleaver was. But there's a decent chance the division is still 70-30 or 60-40 in favor of the mom being the primary parent, and vice versa for the dad being the primary earner. Consequently, with the typical American couple in front of a court seeking a divorce—one of my colleagues, borrowing from *The Simpsons*, calls them Joe Meatball and Sally Housecoat—a judge is going to need to be shown how things are different, or how they have changed.

If you want custody of your kids, you've got to be up front with your lawyer in determining your priorities and setting goals. Don't try to fool yourself or your lawyer. If going to that business meeting on Wednesday afternoon is more important to you than Junior's game, that's okay. Just tell us. As a lawyer, I am dependent on you, and on the information you give me. Your role as a parent in the custody considerations is going to be diminished only if you allow it to be diminished. You're not irrelevant, no matter what the stereotypes say.

Bart came to us a few years ago, very hurt and angry that his wife, a stay-at-home mom, had found a new guy and wanted a divorce. They had five kids, and to take care of the kids and a nonworking wife, Bart was working overtime at a local factory.

"I want custody of my kids," Bart told me.

"How are you going to do that?" I asked. "You worked seven days last week, more than sixty hours in all. When you were home you ate and slept. You didn't even see your kids. How are you going to be the primary parent and take care of the kids?"

Bart hadn't thought that through. We started talking about how much time his wife spent in the kitchen and shopping for groceries and doing laundry and supervising homework and driving kids around. He didn't have much to say. Then we talked about how many hours he could work around all that duty, and what it would mean to live on his straight wages—no overtime, 40 hours a week—for long periods. We talked about what it would cost to bring in household help, a cleaner, and babysitters who could cook. "Would it be better for you to have custody and bring in strangers to take care of the kids and the house," I wondered, "or would it be better to let their mom take care of the kids when you are working?" Bart ended up trimming the overtime and working less, but he also ended up trimming his request for primary custody. He and his wife ended up with something like shared custody, though it was a happily flexible arrangement that meant he got to see at least two or three of the kids almost every day, and had all five of them at the same time on alternate weekends.

As lawyers, we need to know what's really important to you, and how much you are willing to give up to achieve that goal. Maybe we can help you find a way to shift the three o'clock meeting so that you don't have to miss the game. Or maybe we can help you figure out ways to do something with Junior other than the game. Maybe everybody is better off if you attend the three o'clock meeting. Maybe you're happier as the primary breadwinner who sees the kids part-time, rather than being stressed out by balancing work and custody, and not doing a very good job at either one. Maybe the kids are better off spending more time with their mom. These conversations with your lawyer are a reality check, a time for dads to make some hard decisions about who they are and what they want to be post-divorce.

There's one other lesson from Bart's case. He wanted custody in part to punish his wife. "She's not a fit mother," he said. "She's committing adultery." It seemed to me that Bart, at least when he first came in, was thinking more of himself than the kids. His wife had hurt him, and he wanted to hurt her by taking the kids away from her. "I understand," I said. "She's cheated on you. But that's not the principal issue on the table. The court is concerned about the structure surrounding the children. Is changing the structure—so your wife is no longer the primary caregiver—going to hurt the kids or help them?" It's a delicate moment for a lawyer. I didn't want to criticize my client, but I wanted to ease him back toward a more realistic perspective so he could look at the situation with emotional intelligence rather than pure emotion.

If a client doesn't know much about how judges decide custody contests—and most clients don't—a good lawyer will

If a client doesn't know much about how judges decide custody contests—and most clients don't—a good lawyer will sit him down and give him a tutorial.

sit him down and give him a tutorial. Let's do that here. One of the interesting things is that many dads believe such decisions are made arbitrarily, because judges are biased in favor of women. But when we break down the various factors going into the decision, clients usually understand and appreciate the deliberations and considerations that face judges. The first thing judges look at is family history. Is that fair? To look at the role each parent has played in raising the kids? It might be painful to admit for someone like Bart, who's been working long hours, but most fathers would agree that, yes, the family history should be a factor.

Naturally, some dads can be quick to claim that they were "equal" parents even if they clearly were not. Sometimes, to make the point, we have to question these clients closely: Who changed diapers more often? Who put the kids to bed? Who got them up? Who took them to the dentist? Who went to parent-teacher conferences? That's parenting, and there is often a record. Events that make up parenting can be quantified and counted. That's the history, pre-breakup, that judges consider. Fortunately for dads who don't have a long history of sterling parenting while their marriages were intact, the courts can and often do consider an even more important factor: the future.

The moment of a breakup can be seen as a time for a fresh start. You're splitting up, you're getting divorced, and like it or not, things are changing. It's an opportunity to change your parenting role, particularly if you want more custody and your soon-to-be-ex's role is changing too. We've seen studies that indicate that a great many of the men who get divorced in their thirties and into their forties are getting divorced because their wives want to, not because they want to. An all-too-common scenario—we've seen it literally thousands of times, all across the country—is that the wife is getting close to her fortieth birthday, she feels like she's getting trapped in the role of a mom, and she feels like her husband is taking her for granted. She meets someone new who is exciting and gives her the sort of attention that her husband used to give her. Eventually she wants to start over with the new boyfriend, so she tells her husband she wants a divorce.

The husband, our client, didn't ask for any of this. He wants things to keep going the way they have been. But things are never going to be the same. His illusion of control is gone. He's got to deal with it. He's been a good dad, involved but not overly involved. He's always worked long and hard, and traveled sometimes for business. But now he wants joint custody. But his wife has always been the primary caregiver. She had a part-time job—that's where she met the boyfriend—but that was mostly while the kids were in school. So she has the advantage in the custody contest in terms of family history. She's been the main parent at home.

Our client, however, can seize change as an opportunity. Maybe his soon-to-be-ex's situation has changed. Instead of being focused on hearth and home, maybe her new relationship is her new focus. Maybe she's more concerned about spending time with her new beau than about whether her kids have their homework done every night. Maybe she's moved out and doesn't have a place of her own. Maybe she's short on money and needs to get a job. Maybe her life isn't quite as stable as it was, and maybe she isn't quite the rock of the family that she once was.

Perhaps the dad, our client, is making some changes too. Maybe he's cut back on his workload. Maybe he's doing a lot of the things that his soon-to-be-ex used to do for the kids.

Maybe he's becoming the stable one, the one the kids look to when they skin a knee or they're getting bullied at school. The courts value stability of routine and community as important for kids. Going through a divorce is usually the most difficult thing young kids have ever faced. Their world is falling apart, or being torn apart by the two people they love and trust the most. That's why it's important to buttress the kids' emotional fragility with as few additional changes as possible. Courts like to see kids stay in the same house or at least the same neighborhood. They like to see kids go to the same school and hang out with the same friends. Moving to a new city and changing schools in mid-divorce does not contribute to a kid's stability. If the dad can offer more stability, that's a huge plus. History is significant in a custody contest, but the here and now—and the future—can be even more important.

Beyond past and future family roles, my tutorial for dads embarking on a custody contest touches on two other factors that can be important. One pertains primarily to older kids: Whom do they want to live with? I think everybody agrees that kids should be heard and their opinions considered. But sometimes kids' preferences should be taken with a grain of salt. Earlier we discussed the client whose 16-year-old son wanted to live with Dad; the judge was fine with that until it emerged that Dad was a marijuana dealer. Also, mothers have been known to coach their kids to dislike the dad, especially if she has primary custody during the divorce proceedings.

That leads to another factor that judges sometimes consider: alienation. Judges want everybody to get along. If one parent trash-talks about the other, and it alienates the kids toward the other parent, judges often try to give the wronged parent a chance to start over and make it up with the kids. Sometimes that means more custody for the wronged parent. The reasoning, of course, is that the kids are smart enough to make up their own minds if they have a chance to get to know both parents and aren't being brainwashed by one against the other. It's an important lesson for dads to remember: Part of your duty during the divorce proceedings, and well after the ink has dried on the divorce decree, is to protect both parents' relationships with the kids. It's part of providing a stable, healthy environment for the kids.

Part of your duty during the divorce proceedings, and well after the ink has dried on the divorce decree, is to protect both parents' relationships with the kids.

When planning your case with your lawyer, think of it as building a wall, brick by brick. Some bricks are going to be big, some small. But you need to keep piling them up until your case is a big strong wall that is difficult for your soon-to-be-ex to knock down.

A wife's misconduct can be a big brick: mistreating the kids, drinking too much, mental instability, taking off with the kids. The dad's everyday actions can be small bricks: tucking the kids in, making sure they have clean clothes, taking them to the doctor. Some dads walk into our offices with their walls already built. One of our lawyers had a recent case involving a stay-at-home dad who did everything that June Cleaver did, except without the pearls. His wife ran an executive search company for the hospitality industry, and was always flying around the country as a headhunter recruiting managers for five-star resorts. They were each good at their roles. She made a lot of money, and he loved nothing better than taking care of the house and their six-year-old twins. But she found herself getting bored coming back to this homebody. She was used to fine wines and gourmet food and luxurious spas. She was used to working with people who talked about world affairs and large commercial developments and million-dollar deals. She'd come home to meat loaf and excruciating details about which twin had lost which tooth and how much the tooth fairy had left under her pillow.

The at-home dad hired one of the very accomplished women attorneys in our firm. When they first went to court for the hearing for temporary orders, to determine money and custody while the divorce was pending, our lawyer could tell that the judge—a man, and a traditionalist who had been on the bench for decades—was uncomfortable with the idea of our client requesting residential custody and a substantial amount of money each month. Our lawyer realized she had to address role reversal, the 500-pound gorilla in the courtroom. During a conference in chambers she said, "Your Honor, with all due respect, I'd suggest that you look at my client as if he was wearing a dress." The judge just stared at her for a second through his rimless glass, and then a wave of recognition came over his face. He didn't say anything except, "Mmm. Thank you." But he got it. The judge embraced the role reversal, and our housedad got the same sort of temporary order that his wife would have gotten if she had been the stay-at-home mom and he had been the globetrotting executive.

Even dads who don't stay at home full-time with the kids occasionally walk into our office with lots of small bricks in the wall they are building. They are naturally engaged, involved dads. The trouble is that sometimes, because of the stereotype, people don't believe it when a dad says he is really involved. It's the old double standard again. Nobody, including a judge, seems to doubt it when a mom says that she makes sure the kids brush their teeth every night, and that she reads them a story till they fall asleep. If a guy says that, people raise their eyebrows. Really? He reads to his kids instead of watching *SportsCenter* highlights? C'mon.

A wife's attorney has a surefire way of attacking a dad who claims to be more involved than he is. The lawyer simply starts asking questions about the kids: What time does Jack get up? What color is Jill's favorite sweater? What kind of breakfast cereal do they like? What kind of toothpaste did your dentist recommend for them?

Most dads working eight, nine, ten hours a day aren't going to know all that stuff. They appear to be less involved than they claimed, and sometimes clueless, especially if they don't know the names of their kids' teachers or their kids' friends. That line of questioning by an opposing counsel can be devastating. We had one client—he turned out to be a real blowhard—who insisted that he had done everything with his toddler, including taking the kid to day care every morning. Yeah, he said, the staff knew him really well. But when the opposing attorney put the director of the day care center on the stand and asked her to identify the guy, she looked around the courtroom, confused. She couldn't pick him out.

In contrast, one of my all-time-favorite days in court was when the opposing lawyer attacked my client by asking for details of the kids' lives—and my guy knew everything. He knew that his little guy loved his SpongeBob underwear during the day and had to have on his Power Rangers pajamas at night. He knew that the big sister was struggling with finding the right group of friends in middle school. Before long the other lawyer was looking back at his client, the mom, with his eyebrows raised, as if saying, hey, why didn't you give me something he wouldn't know? It didn't matter, my client knew everything. He was a superstar on the stand.

If a dad isn't as involved with the kids as he says, maybe he shouldn't get as much custody as he wants. Our office had a custody contest recently where two kids were going back and forth separately between the estranged parents. The 15-year-old boy would be with the mom when the 13-year-old girl was with the dad, and vice versa. The kids were never together and neither parent ever had both kids at once—or a night off. Our client was clearly worn down. He had been used to his wife taking care of the kids. Now all of a sudden he was on duty for child care every night—and still working his usual 50 hours a week. Under questioning, he seemed unclear about who needed to be where on what afternoons, who was having trouble with which subjects in school, and whom his kids were hanging out with. On top of it all, our attorney could tell that the girl apparently didn't take showers or brush her hair when she stayed with dad. The poor guy thought he could take it all on and do it all, but he couldn't. He seemed disappointed but resigned to the fact when the judge rejected his request for residential custody and ruled that the kids should live primarily with the ex-wife.

MAKING YOURSELF THE BEST CHOICE

So what can you as a dad do when facing divorce, either before the actual breakup or as soon as it happens, to improve your position in a looming custody battle? If you are not already involved with your kids, you should become involved. If you think you're already super-involved, you should become even more involved. Here's the first thing to do: Get to know the kids' schedules. What time do they wake up? What time does school start? When are

their music lessons and sports practices? Is there a set time for homework
after school? For playing? What time
do they go to bed?

That's a start. Then fill in the gaps.
What do they like for breakfast? When
do they brush their teeth? Who makes
their lunches? What do they like for snacks? What are their best
subjects in school? What are their friends' names, and what do
they do when they go over to their homes to play? How much
time do they spend in front of the computer?

*If you are not already
involved with your
kids, you should
become involved. If you
think you're already
super-involved, you
should become even
more involved.*

Learning all this is a win-win situation. Yes, you're doing it
because you want custody. But the only way to glean all this
information is to spend a lot of time with the kids, talking to
them, interacting with them. You're going to find out a lot about
them—and yourself. You're going to become closer to them and
you're going to become a better dad. If you think you can do
that by continuing the same patterns and playing the same role
that you've always played in your marriage and in your family life,
you're probably going to end up seeing your kids no more than
you did before.

If you travel a lot and your expectation is just that whenever you come home you're going to be with the kids, that may
be rather naïve. You're probably going to have, depending on
how complex your divorce is, a pretty set schedule. The less you
travel, the better off you'll be. That can present a quandary, of
course: If you work less or travel less, you're probably going to
make less money. And then you're not going to be able to pay
your child support or alimony. Some judges will take reduced
income into consideration, and reduce your financial obligations
if you're earning less in order to spend more time with the kids.

Ex-wives often claim that a dad is earning less simply so he won't have to pay her more every month; the burden of proving otherwise often falls on the man. One of my clients actually changed to a less demanding job and took a $20,000 pay cut to be with his kids, but we still had to present a weekly schedule, before the breakup and after, showing that he really was spending more time with the kids, and the only way he could do it was by working less.

Don't go into a custody battle with broad-brush generalizations: "She's a lousy mother" or "I'm by far the better parent." The legal system is driven by evidence and proof. The more evidence you have, the better chance of getting the results you want. Let's start with the big bricks, the glaring misconduct on the part of the mom. If she hits the kids, document it. If she misses appointments, make notes. If she exhibits erratic behavior, describe it on paper. If she is talking crazy, flip on a tape recorder. If she gets drunk, take a video of her. Those are big bricks in the wall you're building. Keep a log. One of the most common fact patterns we see is the guy who comes in and says, "I need to get custody because my wife is an alcoholic." Okay, we say, who watches the kids when you are at work?

"Uh," he says. "She does."

We explain that if he's going to claim he can't leave the kids with his wife, he has to stop leaving the kids with his wife. He needs to get babysitters or day care or put them in an after-school program or send them to his mother's or do something to show that he really can't leave them with her, even if she is home full-time. If he knows the kids are in harm's way, it's his obligation to protect them—no matter how much it costs to hire a babysitter or put a kid in day care. We need evidence that he should be the residential parent.

Small bricks are important, too. Keep a log of everything you do with the kids, every day. Note when you take them to school and pick them up, when you make them meals, when you supervise baths, when you help with homework. Take them to doctors' appointments. Make sure you speak to the doctor and the staff notes that you were there. Help your kids with their homework, and sign their homework books or initial their homework every night. (Many schools have homework books, listing assignments. In once recent case, the deciding factor in a custody contest was the homework book. There were dozens of homework assignments, and the mom had signed for only three. The dad had signed for the rest.) Go to parent-teacher conferences. Even if no conference is scheduled, make sure your kids' teachers see you picking them up, and pop in to talk to teachers. Make sure they get used to seeing you. On the computer, you can set up an Outlook or Google calendar and simply keep track of how much time you spend with the kids each day: picked kids up, made spaghetti for dinner, helped with homework, went out for ice cream before bedtime. That can make a powerful exhibit for the court, as objective evidence of your involvement. Our firm offers our clients an online calendaring program that they can access from anywhere—home, work, on the road—to record events.

If your soon-to-be-ex is falling down on the parenting job, create a paper trail or e-mail trail. Send notes asking why the kid missed a scout meeting or a sports activity or a play rehearsal. Start e-mailing regularly to remind her of the kids' schedules. "Don't forget again—she has piano lessons on Thursday afternoon."

> *If your soon-to-be-ex is falling down on the parenting job, create a paper trail or e-mail trail.*

The old double standard still comes into play during divorce proceedings, and it can both cause problems and present opportunities for dads. Moms sometimes buy into the stereotype, especially when it's convenient for them. "I had that kid, I gave birth, that kid is mine," they tell themselves. "My husband, soon to be ex, is paying the child support just to rent the kid out for the weekend. I can do whatever I want with the kid." So the mom takes the kid out of town when it's the dad's weekend, or fails to bring the kid to the dad at the appointed hour. Maybe she refuses to co-parent; she may or may not tell the dad that the kid has a doctor's appointment, and then may or may not tell him about the results. She keeps the kid home from school without checking with him. Or she decides the kid isn't feeling well and keeps the kid home even though it's the dad's night, and the dad would be happy to take care of the kid even if he or she isn't feeling well.

This can be frustrating, to the point of infuriating. "It's unfortunate," we tell our clients, "but you've got to live with it. Sometimes it's part of divorce. Take the high ground." We advise dads to express their disappointment. They shouldn't simply accept their soon-to-be-ex's misbehavior, but neither should they yell or scream or throw a fit. You've gained nothing and lost everything if you give her an excuse to call the cops. Again, keep a journal, and note when she falls down on the job. One mistake some dads make is to complain when their soon-to-be-exes "dump" the kids on them: "It was supposed to be her weekend, but instead she asked me to take the kids so she could go skiing." They scribble it down in their journals as further evidence of how the mom is ignoring court orders. Hold on, we tell our clients. This is another opportunity. Go ahead and note it in your custody journal, but in a positive light. You were able to do more with the kids. You changed your plans—maybe you broke a date with a new lady or maybe you gave up a night out with the guys—to spend more time with your kids. On paper, it's power-ful. Your soon-to-be-ex gave up a chance to be with the kids and you seized the day. Put the time with the kids ahead of the fact that she is doing something wrong.

One last example of a client who took our advice: He and his wife were young, only in their mid-twenties, when he came to us. They already had two little kids, a boy and a girl. Both the husband and wife worked. He was a salesman for a small manu-facturing company and she was an administrative assistant in an insurance agency. The mom wanted sole custody and he wanted joint custody, equal time. The problem was that the client had always let his wife do most of the parenting. He admitted it. He played a lot of golf as part of his job, including on weekends, and he often went out with customers afterward to the nineteenth hole.

We urged him to cut back on the golf and the extracurricular activities, and to get more involved with the kids: drop them off and pick them up from day care; get to know the day care staff, and talk to them about the kids; get to know the other par-ents, and set up playdates, home and away from home; take the kids to their doctors' appointments; enroll them and take them to weekend enrichment classes at the local YMCA. All that and more; everything we suggested to the client, he did it. He'd come in and ask us, "What more can I do?" We had just about run out of things to suggest by the time we got to trial, even though we had agreed with our client not to push for a quick trial date. Usually men want an early trial date so that they can get it over with and set the divorce behind them and start their lives anew. But in this case, as part of our strategy, we let the proceedings go on longer in order to give our client more time to build his wall—and document what a good parent he was.

By the time we got to trial, he had voluminous records—evidence—of his involvement. Judges are used to seeing dads who come to court after stepping up their involvement with the kids for only a few weeks. This client had been at it, nonstop, for ten months. The judge could see he was a committed, involved parent. His soon-to-be-ex and her lawyer bought into the old double standard, assuming she somehow had a natural right to the kids. They didn't have nearly the documentation that our client did.

In the end, the judge said he had rarely seen such an involved parent, and that keeping the kids away from their dad would cause them substantial harm. The judge ruled for 50-50 joint custody for our client, and he was ecstatic. You know how we say nobody wins in a divorce case? That was the exception that proves the rule. It was a win. And it remains a shining example of a dad who came in, laid out his priorities, worked out a plan with his lawyer, and then executed the plan. There was never any guarantee—the judge still could have ruled against him and given the mom full custody—but he put himself in a position to get the result he wanted, and that's how it turned out.

DON'T MAKE A STUPID MISTAKE:
BE INVOLVED WITH YOUR KIDS.

DOING A SLOPPY JOB ON FINANCIAL RECORDS

CLINTON WAS AN engineer, an aerospace engineer who worked for a company that develops computerized navigation systems for jetliners. He was a slender guy who dressed sensibly, ate healthfully, averaged two beers a week, went to the gym regularly, served on committees at his church, and volunteered at a homeless shelter. With his glasses and the little belt holster for his cell phone, he looked like a nerd. "I might not be colorful, but I'm not boring," he told our lawyer. His wife apparently disagreed. Clinton came to one of our lawyers for an initial consultation after his wife said she needed a lot more excitement in her life—and a lot less Clinton.

Both in their early forties, they had been married six years and didn't have any kids, so Clinton thought the divorce would be pretty cut and dried. A simple equation: He'd keep what was his, she'd keep what was hers, and they'd split up the rest evenly.

She had different ideas. She was happy not to have to share any-thing with Clinton from the trust fund her parents had left her to educate their kids, if they ever had any. But she insisted that she get half of a 401(k) that Clinton had from his first job, when he was in his twenties. He had gotten a good job out of engineer-ing school, and had started making decent money right away. Careful guy that he was, Clinton started putting the max into the retirement fund from his very first paycheck. His first employer had matched his contributions. By the time he left that first en-gineering job to go work on jetliner navigation systems, Clinton had a nice tidy sum—six figures—in the account.

While he was still in his twenties and working at that first job, Clinton also invested in a rental property, buying a duplex in a nice neighborhood. It didn't take a lot of work on his part, he always seemed to find reliable tenants, and he made good money on the investment.

During the divorce, his wife said that she deserved half of what was in the 401(k) and half the value of the rental property because some of the worth—from rising investments and prop-erty values—had come during their years together.

Clinton wasn't the sort of guy to get angry, but he didn't like that his soon-to-be-ex-wife was trying to take what clearly was not hers. He was more than a little peeved that his wife was dumping him, and he didn't feel obliged to finance her new excitement. Most guys would simply have moaned about how that wasn't fair, and called her selfish and much worse. Typically, our lawyers ask our clients to disprove what the wife was saying—present evidence that she didn't have anything to do with the retirement account or the rental property. Most guys would grumble and say they'd try to find some records, and then do little or nothing.

They'd end up losing some of the assets because they didn't have records to fight the other side's claim.

Not Clinton. Like many engineers—and military people, who also seem to be highly organized—Clinton had the records and the evidence. He produced every bit of paper related to that retirement account. He showed all the withholdings from his checks, all the employer's contributions, and monthly statements showing how the account increased in value. He produced the paperwork from the former employer showing the date that he left, and a copy of the individual investments within the account with their respective values on that day. He produced records showing how the investments had climbed over the years. Clinton's record keeping made our job much easier; we did not have to track down investment firm or employer records to determine the values of the investments at various points in time.

Even more remarkable, Clinton produced the original records from the checking account that was devoted solely to his duplex business—cash flow in and out. His deposits into the account matched to the penny his expenses for the duplex. He had opened the checking account when he bought the duplex, before he met his wife. His name was the only name that had ever been on the account, and every nickel that went into or came from that account had been signed for by Clinton only. He had a work log showing what repairs, maintenance, and other work he had done himself or paid contractors to do for the duplex. When it snowed, he usually went over and personally shoveled the snow off the sidewalk in front of the duplex. He'd write that down in his log. If he was out of town when it snowed, he had a neighborhood teenager do the shoveling for $20, and he noted that in his log, too. Nowhere in the log was his wife mentioned, except once—the time his car had been in the shop and she had dropped him off on a Saturday afternoon to start regrouting the shower stall in one of the apartments. The duplex was only a few blocks from their house, so he had walked home.

Just to make sure everyone knew the exact date he had met his wife, he produced copies of their first e-mails back and forth after they were matched up through an online dating service.

Clinton's financial records were a lawyer's dream. Our attorney used those records to show not only that Clinton had the 401(k) and the duplex before the marriage, but that he had kept sole control of the assets during the marriage. Furthermore, his records showed that his wife had absolutely nothing to do with the duplex. If she had been able to show that she had invested time or money in the upkeep of the duplex, she might have had an argument. But she couldn't.

THE IMPORTANCE OF ORDER

Clinton, obviously, WAS an exception to the typical guy who comes to us for help. Most men think of financial records as an annoying technicality they've got to endure. So they fill out the forms haphazardly, guessing and leaving blanks. "Close enough is good enough," one client complained when we asked him to go back and do a better job. He told us he had filled out the forms while watching football on a Sunday afternoon. He was finished with the forms by the time the whistle blew ending the first quarter. The impression among many men is that the financial statement is simply some background for their lawyer; they think the records will be filed away somewhere and will have no significant impact on their lives. That is so wrong. Exactly the opposite is true. Those financial forms are going to determine how much child support and maintenance the man pays his wife, both during the divorce proceedings and then when she is officially his ex-wife. Those financial forms are also going to determine how much of their assets—house, car, savings, investments—he will retain

Financial forms will determine how much child support and maintenance you pay your wife, both during the divorce proceedings and then when she is officially your ex-wife.

and how much will walk out the door with his wife. Those financial forms are probably going to determine what kind of lifestyle the client is going to have after the divorce, and maybe what the entire rest of his life is going to be like.

One of the things we do with clients is sit them down and have a meeting on finances. We explain the two big reasons they should give the financial forms their full attention. If you don't do as good a job on the financial records as possible, two things can happen. One, you've done yourself harm by basically giving away some of your money to your soon-to-be-ex. Money that would have been in your pocket will be in her pocketbook instead. Depending on how badly you muck up the financial records, it could be a little money or it could be a lot. Either way, it could have been yours, and instead it will be hers.

The second bad thing that can happen is that sloppy financial reporting can hurt your credibility during the divorce proceedings. If your financial reports are haphazard or incomplete, the judge hearing your divorce case is going to think you don't care very much about the terms of the final decree. If you put down numbers that your soon-to-be-ex's attorney can prove are false, the judge may regard you as deceitful. The judge may reason, well, if this guy is lying about his financial records, what else is he lying about? The damage to your credibility can not only hurt your financial status, but it can also color the judge's thinking in terms of custody. We'll discuss this in more detail below, but here's the takeaway for now: If you do a poor job on your financial records, you might end up not having as much money or as much time with your kids as you had hoped.

Putting together your financial records is one of those grubby jobs that are really worth doing right the first time. Remember, the financial records filed with the court are a sworn statement: You're swearing to tell the truth, the whole truth, and nothing but the truth in those financial reports. You're not swearing to sort of take a guess during football commercials at what you think the numbers might be. Yeah, you may think you can turn in guesstimates now and go back and put in the exact numbers later, before the trial; some lawyers will tell you that's okay. But what if you're way off on a number? Suppose you initially estimate that there's $20,000 in a savings account, but you didn't know that your wife had been sneaking money out of the account for months, and when it comes time to revise your financial documents you are surprised to learn that the account has only $5,000 in it. Her lawyer gets you on the stand and challenges your figures: "You say that the account had $20,000 in it, even though now you say it has $5,000, but you didn't take anything out. How do you explain that discrepancy?" The implication will be that it is you, not her, who has skimmed or hidden money. Even if you can prove it was her, you look like a guy who simply wasn't paying attention.

Avoid using estimates. Every number should be based on source documents, if at all possible. If you think you spend $60 on gas every month, don't just write down $60. Go back through your receipts and credit card bills. You can bet that the opposing attorney is going to subpoena your source documents, so you might as well get them together and use them yourself. If you make estimates instead of using the real receipts and records, then the opposing lawyer can ask why. If you had the documents, why didn't you use them? If you don't have them, you look sloppy and disorganized, and your numbers are unreliable.

Don't be tempted to round up or down. Do the arithmetic. (We sometimes joke that if more people knew there was going to be math involved, they might reconsider divorce.) For example, we once had a client say that his electric bill was $200 a month. He had guessed at it. We had him call the electric company, get his bills for each of the previous 12 months, add them up, and then average them. It turned out his average bill for the previous year was $177.28. That might not seem like a big deal—the difference is only $266 for the year—but having the exact figures gave his statement more credibility, and took away the opposing attorney's opportunity to put him on the stand and get him to admit that he had overestimated at least one of his expenses. Then the attorney would ask, "Is it possible, sir, that you have also overestimated some of your other expenses on this form?"

In the earlier discussion about finding the right lawyer, we mentioned the importance of a team approach, lawyer and client helping each other, both contributing to the case. Nowhere is that teamwork more critical than here, when pulling together the financial statements. When you're looking for a lawyer, ask lawyers you interview how they handle financial documents. Some lawyers may make it seem simple. They give you some forms, you take them home and fill them out, and you bring them back. While there may be some appeal to that seemingly simple approach, it can be dangerous. Some lawyers simply photocopy the handwritten numbers that their clients filled in, and give that to the court. That kind of quick, sloppy work sends a real message to the judge: This lawyer isn't very professional, and this client doesn't care very much about the process or what is going to happen to him. Ask about what happens when you turn in your handwritten numbers. Are they simply photocopied? Are they simply retyped into a form? Or are they incorporated into a sophisticated spreadsheet?

When you are interviewing lawyers, make sure you get a lawyer who will go through the numbers with you, or have an experienced paralegal do it. You want them to push you and nail down the source of each number, and they can do that only by going through your forms with you.

Our lawyers go over the numbers with each client—as every lawyer should do with every client—and go over the financial statements number by number. We want the client to be sure the numbers are accurate, and we want to be sure. We'll often point out missing numbers and ask our clients to go back and fill in the blanks. If they don't have the original documents to explain how they got to a number, we tell them to go look again. "We know you're busy, and we know this isn't the happiest chore anyone has ever asked you to do," we tell our clients. "But you've hired us to represent you, and get you the best outcome, and to protect you. If you don't want to do the legwork yourself, we'll have a legal assistant run the credit records for you. Give us the authorization, and we'll gather your financial records and go through them for you. But you cannot just ignore the financial aspects of the case. We need that information."

Here's the level of detail we want: Are you taking your kids to McDonald's a couple of times a week and spending $20 each time? Or are you going out with buddies after work every Thursday night at Hooters and spending $200 on shots, wings, and tips? We're not going to tell you how to live your life, but we may well tell you to at least pay cash at Hooters, rather than putting those charges on your credit card.

When a client says all that information can't possibly be important, we agree. "You're absolutely right," we say. "Ninety percent of the financial information we pull together—maybe more—is not going to have any influence on the case. But ten percent of the information we gather will dictate how you live the rest of your life. What kind of place you live in. What kind of car you drive. What kind of vacations you take. And how much money you have to spend on your kids."

> *Ninety percent of the financial information we pull together is not going to have any influence on the case. But ten percent of the information we gather will dictate how you live the rest of your life.*

Our clients ponder this for a moment, and then we say, "But can you tell us which 90 percent doesn't matter and which 10 percent does? No? Well, as lawyers, neither can we. We can't tell in advance what is going to be important. That's why we need to do a good job on everything, because any of it could make the difference between whether you spend the next five years in a nice house that you own or a crummy little apartment that you rent."

A lot of working-class guys come to us thinking they don't have to pay attention to the money because they don't have any. They don't earn a lot. They don't have many assets, and they've got at least as much in debt. "This is gonna be an easy breakup. We don't have kids. We haven't been married long. What's hers is hers and what's mine is mine," they say. Sometimes these clients say, "I don't need to fill out a separate financial report. I'll just go along with whatever hers says. Both of our documents are going to be the same, so what's the big deal?"

They think that not being wealthy means they are going to have a quick, cheap, uncomplicated divorce. And sometimes that happens. But we've seen a lot of $700 divorces blow up into $7,000 divorces when the man and woman suddenly can't agree on the numbers. Sometimes she agrees with only half of the equation, and she thinks what's hers is hers, and what's his is hers, too. A lot of men are surprised to find out that their wives have been saving or spending money they didn't know about.

In almost every case, whether the people are rich or poor, we suggest a couple of things to clients during our first discussion about money. One is a credit check. A common surprise is for a man to find out that his wife has taken out credit cards he didn't know about—in both their names. Another issue may be that she hasn't been writing the checks for loans she was supposed to be paying off. To help get the big picture and sniff out details, we always urge our clients to run their credit reports. There are how-to articles on our website, www.dadsdivorce.com, about how to run credit checks inexpensively or even for free. You (and we) need to know the real financial picture, not what you hope it is.

Another thing we suggest, if the client hasn't started doing it already, is to begin untangling and separating his finances from his wife's. You and your soon-to-be-ex should no longer be sharing a credit card account. You might want to keep the joint checking account for paying household bills, but you should set up your own individual bank accounts, too, in a different bank. Most bank deposit agreements allow the bank to move money from your individual account to your joint account to cover your wife's overdrafts. In some smaller communities, the bank may even move money out of your individual account on your wife's request since they know you are spouses. By using an entirely different bank you limit or avoid such involuntary transfers.

Sometimes it is permissible—check with your lawyer first—to take your half of the money out of a savings or investment account at the start of the divorce proceedings. But don't loot an account by cleaning it out; if you wife does that, document it right away, and make sure your lawyer knows about it right away. If you have joint investment accounts, confirm with the brokerage that both parties must sign for any withdrawals to prevent her from draining the account and creating additional tax consequences.

In most jurisdictions, people involved in a divorce have to fill out forms that show (a) their income and expenditures and (b) their assets and debts. Sometimes the two financial categories are separate forms, and sometimes they are combined into one form. The income and expenditures form tracks money flowing in and out for the husband, the wife, and the combined household. The assets and debts form, also called a balance sheet, looks at what he owns, what she owns, and what they own together. The balance sheet also looks at their debts—what he owes, what she owes, and what they owe together. At the bottom of the sheet the debts are subtracted from the assets to show what is owned, and by whom. The figures on these documents will be scrutinized, checked, and perhaps challenged by the attorneys and maybe the judge. The numbers will decide the division of property—who walks away with what out of the marriage. The numbers will also decide the ongoing maintenance and support payments—who pays how much to whom each month.

Let's look at the income and expenses part of the financial statements. The typical client is a W-2 earner who earns everything from a single employer. That's pretty cut and dried for the lawyer. But more and more of us these days moonlight or freelance in one way or another. And more and more of us have our own businesses, whether it's the main thing we do or something on the side. Men who have businesses—whether they have an office or a shop with employees, or simply pick up a little spending money doing odds and ends—have much more complicated financial obligations and opportunities. There are many more chances to write off expenses, and to declare property as capital assets. If you run a business, large or small, talk to your lawyer in detail about it, and don't hesitate to follow the lawyer's advice about bringing in accountants, tax advisors, appraisers, and other financial experts. In terms of income, essentially what the courts are looking for is your meaningful, disposable income— the money you bring home that you can and do spend on yourself and your family.

Expenses are probably the area of the financial statements that both parties screw up most often. You should come up with a detailed profile of your personal expenses, your combined household expenses, and your wife's expenses. You may have to guess at some of these, but you'd be surprised how much you can get from credit card or debit card records. You also need to document your income, her income, and your combined income, if any (from jointly held investments, for example). The court is going to look at the bottom line for each of you: what you have left after subtracting your expenses from your income, and the same for your wife.

We often tell clients to go back and add up all their expenses over a year, and then divide by twelve to get their monthly expenses. Lawyers love it when a guy comes in with everything already recorded on Quicken or some other computerized database, but most men aren't that organized. If making lists on notepaper is the best you can do, no problem. But do your best.

* * *

FOR THE INCOME and expenses part of the financial statement, you want your bottom-line figure to be as low as possible, and you want hers to be as high as possible. That's because the judge is going to look at each side's bottom line in deciding maintenance and child support payments. The higher your bottom line, the more money you have that the judge can award to your soon-to-be-ex. The lower the bottom line, the less there is for her. And the opposite is true for her: The lower her income and the higher her expenses, the more she is going to need from you. If there is a range of potential income and expenses, year to year or month to month, lean to the side of your lowest income and your maximum expenses. As long as you are within what lawyers call the range of truthfulness or honesty, and you can back it up with source documents, you are okay. "The judge is going to be looking for extra money to give her," we warn our clients. "The perfect financial statement for a client would show he is just barely covering his expenses, or maybe even be in the hole a little bit in a typical month."

> *For the income and expenses part of the financial statement, you want your bottom-line figure to be as low as possible, and you want hers to be as high as possible.*

We try hard to make sure clients don't miss any of their expenses. It's rare for a client to bring us his financial statement and not have to add something he's forgotten. Clients often miss expenses such as gifts, pet food and supplies, newspaper and magazine subscriptions, phone plans, gym or health club memberships, eyeglasses, vitamins, and prescription medication. Look for money that comes out of your check automatically, such as union dues, vacation savings, or college tuition invest-ment programs. Think about everything you spend, every nickel. Do you stop and get a cup of coffee and a donut every day on the way to work? That may not seem like much, but it's probably $60 a month, and if you forget to list it, you could end up paying your wife $30 more a month than you need to pay.

Don't feel obliged to hold down your expenses so you'll look like a good guy. The judge doesn't care how good you are with money. I once saw a guy—not one of my clients—fill out fi-nancial statements showing he earned $10,000 a month but had expenses of only $3,000 a month. When he got on the stand and told the judge he was broke, the judge was incredulous. The ex-wife, of course, did very well in terms of alimony in that case. Remember, we want your expenses to be toward the high end of that honesty range because otherwise you'll end up with "extra" money at the end of the month, and judges look for extra money to award to ex-wives.

Food is always a wild card, because so many men can't recall everything they spend, and there is such a range of what indi-viduals spend—or think they spend—on food. Most men, out on their own, will spend about $250 a month on food, maybe a little less if they live in small towns, but maybe $300 or more if they live in big cities. I once had a client who claimed he spent $600 a month on food.

"The judge is going to notice that," I warned the client.

"I was married 23 years," he said. "I never cooked a meal. Now I eat out every meal. It's costing me $600 a month, believe me." I believed him, and after I had him start keeping all his restaurant receipts, the judge believed him, too.

On the other hand, I once had a client who said he was

spending only $80 a month on food. "What," I asked, "are you some kind of monk?"

"Nah," he said, laughing. "I'm just cheap. I hate to spend more than I have to on anything. I buy all my food at Costco. Plain, simple stuff. I buy almost all my food in bulk, when it's on sale, and I keep the perishable stuff in two big freezers. I cook everything myself."

Men often forget or underestimate their spending on clothes, probably because most of us go shopping for clothes maybe once a year. Women, in contrast, seem to shop more often. So go back through your spending for an entire year—yes, really, the entire previous year—and add up all the expenses. If you look back only three months but you bought all your clothes for the year six months ago, you're going to miss that expense—and half of it will go to your ex-wife.

The same thing with expenditures such as household maintenance and repairs. Maybe you have a snowplow come in the winter; you won't include that expense if you look only at your records for April through September. The same with a lawn service; you might pay for it only during the warm months, but you'll want to count that in your monthly expenses over the entire year. Look even farther back, two or three years, in terms of household maintenance and repair. Maybe you didn't spend anything on the house last year, but over the previous two years you've paid $4,000 for renovations and repairs. That figures out to more than $100 a month in expenses that you'll want to include. Other expenses that are often overlooked or miscalculated include heating and cooling bills that go up and down with the seasons, quarterly water bills, and semiannual auto and life insurance premiums.

Clients also need to discuss their future expenses with their attorneys—how their expenses might change when the divorce is final. Try to make a forward projection. For example, you might be driving one of the two family vehicles. The one you are driving is paid off, but the one your soon-to-be-ex is driving is not. If you are going to be switching cars, or you are going to need a new car in the foreseeable future, you should factor that into your financial statements. "Keep an eye on the future," I tell clients. Clients need to let us know if they're going to be taking on additional expenses at any time, such as kids going to private school next year or needing braces in a couple of years.

Many men who move out end up living temporarily with relatives or friends. They'll crash in a spare bedroom or in the basement rec room. "Just till the divorce is taken care of," they reason. "Then I'll know what I can afford, and I can go look for a permanent place." The rationale is sound, but we often advise men who have moved out to go ahead and rent a place—as nice a place as they can afford, the kind of place where they might want to live post-divorce. The longer a client lives in a "temporary" situation, the more opposing counsel, and perhaps the judge, will find the "temporary" to be acceptable as the post-divorce arrangement. We want the client to be able to show reasonable housing expenses in his financial statements during the divorce proceedings, along with a reasonable residence for his kids. The amount he spends to put a roof over his head is a solid, concrete number. Without that, if he is living for free or paying a token rent to his parents or a buddy, the soon-to-be-ex's attorney can put forth a much lower rent. The judge could end up accepting that number and telling him that seems reasonable, here's what you're going to have for housing. It's a lot easier to prove what you are paying than to prove what you might have to pay.

Keep an eye on future income, too. You might have gotten used to receiving a nice annual bonus every year. As we've seen in recent years, however, bonuses can evaporate. You shouldn't count on the bonus—and your soon-to-be-ex shouldn't count on getting half of it.

For the assets and debts part of the financial statements, the goal is to assign a lower value to the assets you keep and a higher value to the assets she takes. The biggest joint asset is often the house. You want to get an appraiser, one of your own. If your number for the value of the house is a guess and your wife's number is from an appraiser, which one do you think the judge is going to give more weight? By the same token, if you run a business, get professionals in to value the business—and the future prospects for the business.

When adding up your assets and trying to put a dollar value on each item, try to figure out which ones are most likely to be sold for cash—the things that neither of you will want, most likely. Think about which things you are going to want and which things she is going to want. When you assign a dollar value to each item, you still want to be within the range of honesty that we discussed earlier. But if it is an item she is not going to want, assign the lower value to it. If it is an item she is going to want, assign the higher value to it. The more valuable her stuff and the less valuable your stuff, the less you have to pay for your share of dividing up your assets. You may think your collection of old baseball cards could fetch several thousand dollars on eBay if you sold the cards individually or in small batches, but this isn't the time to be bragging about it. If the guy at the local flea market tells you he wouldn't pay more than $200 for the whole collection, then that's the value you can assign to it on your financial statement. If she's got a collection of thirty antique spoons, on the other hand, you're going to do some research on what the most valuable spoon might be worth, multiply that by 30, and put down that figure on the financial statement.

Don't hesitate to get anything appraised, not only houses and businesses. We had a client whose pride and joy was his Harley-Davidson. He bought it several years earlier for $25,000. Over the years he spent a lot of time and money tricking it out. It was a beauty. He figured that it was worth about $18,000, and that's what he put on his financial statement. His wife said on her statement that it was worth $25,000, because that's what he had paid for it and he had put several thousand more into it. Our client brought in written estimates from two motorcycle shops and an appraiser for a company that insures motorcycles. They all agreed that the resale value of the bike was between $17,800 and $18,500. The judge looked at the wife. What evidence did she have that it was worth $25,000? Her attorney got up and hemmed and hawed and said they didn't really have an appraisal. "But we think the motorcycle should be valued at the original purchase price," the other attorney said, "because he never let her ride on it with him." I'm sure the esteemed opposing counsel had some logic behind that reasoning, but I didn't grasp it, and neither did the judge. The motorcycle went into the books at $18,000.

While we want to make our valuations as favorable as possible, we don't want clients to deliberately mislead the court or conceal material facts. Again, your financial documents are a sworn statement before the court. And while it's rare for anyone to be prosecuted for the crime of perjury after putting down a bad number on a financial statement in a divorce case, it is not unusual for a fudged number to become an embarrassment, usually at the worst possible moment. Yes, you can always say you forgot, or it was an oversight, or it was a typo, but it's still probably going to work against you when the judge makes a final decision. When a judge doesn't like a number, the number typically gets thrown out and the other side's number is the one that is used. We'd rather see our clients file a more reasonable number, and for the judge to split the difference between our number and the other side's number.

IS IT REALLY WORTH IT?

One more point about assets. Yes, we want the numbers to be favorable to us, but we also want to be reasonable, and we want the divorce proceedings to go smoothly for our clients. We want to reach amicable settlements, if we can, in order to avoid expensive, drawn-out trials, and to promote better long-term relations between clients and their ex-wives. Life is simpler if everybody just gets along. But some wives—and some men—get a little crazy when it comes to assigning dollar values to their assets, or deciding who gets what. Sometimes the two sides are more interested in hurting each other than in fairly dividing up their assets.

One of the worst days I ever spent as a lawyer came toward the end of a settlement dispute when neither my client nor his soon-to-be-ex-wife could agree on how to divide up the contents of their house. We finally set up a meeting between me and my client and her and her lawyer. The four of us agreed that they would flip a coin, and whoever won could choose one thing out of the house. Then the other would choose something. They would go back and forth until everything in the house was spoken for.

We flipped a coin and the wife won. My guy grimaced. She smiled, almost an evil smile.

"I choose," she said, pausing to relish the moment, "his collection of shotguns."

My guy exploded, shouting and sputtering. When he calmed down enough to speak, he wore an evil grin too.

"All right, you witch," he said. (Okay, he didn't say witch, but it was a word that's kind of close to witch.) "I'll take the 400-piece antique silver service from your dear old grandmother."

As you might imagine, the day deteriorated from there. They went through the list of items in the household, each choosing not the things they wanted or even the most valuable things, but the things that the other person wanted. It took us eight hours. The man and woman each had to pay a lawyer's fee approaching $2,500 for the privilege of showing just how vindictive they could be. That was the only day in my life that I've ever wished I had studied architecture instead of law.

YOUR SOON-TO-BE-EX and her attorney receive a copy of your financial statement, of course, and we get a copy of hers. They're going to go over your statement, looking for any holes or discrepancies or exaggerations, and we're going to do that to hers. Just as there can be a double standard in custody contests, the financial contest can also be unfair. Right or wrong, courts often view the man as the one in charge, the earner, and his statement is supposed to be complete and flawless. If there are any problems in his statement, the opposing attorney is going to say—and the judge may think—that the guy is being either irresponsible or untruthful. On the other hand, if the woman files a financial statement that isn't up to snuff, everyone is supposed to cut her some slack: After all, she's a busy single mom, she wasn't the primary earner, and she's not the professional.

That doesn't mean we're going to give her a pass on her financial statement. We went over your statement with a fine-tooth comb, and we're going to do the same with hers. One of the first things we'll do, as we did with your statement, is check her arithmetic. We see an amazing number of financial statements from other attorneys that literally don't add up. We'll get out a calculator and add up the individual expenses, and find that the total is higher than it should be. She'll say she needs $200 a month for utilities, and claim that adds up to $3,000 a year. We've seen statements that say in one place that the wife pays $500 a month on her credit card, and in another place that she doesn't have any credit cards. I recall one case where the wife's statement added up everything she needed for a month, and said it was $5,000. But when we added it up, it came to only $2,600. These mistakes can be easily amended, of course, but the mistakes have to go through the court, and give us an opportunity to challenge other parts of the statement, and for the judge to wonder what other mistakes are lurking. We like to put a wife on the stand to defend sloppy statements.

"Ma'am, do you see on the monthly statement where you've listed a motor vehicle registration expense of $65? Is that accurate? You pay $65 every month to the DMV for registration?"

"Oh, no, I must have made a mistake. That should be $65 for the whole year."

"Okay, ma'am, if you look farther down on your financial statement, you estimate $200 a month for automobile service and repairs? We're wondering if that's accurate, given that you drive a brand-new BMW and the warranty covers all service and repairs for the first three years. Is that accurate, ma'am, that $200 a month for automotive repairs?"

"Uh, I guess I made a mistake on that . . ."

We also examine each expense to see if it's reasonable. One woman's statement said she needed $1,650 a month for food—for herself and her two toddlers. Four hundred bucks a week is a lot of food for two parents with two or three hungry teenagers; it's an extraordinary amount for a mom and two little kids, especially when the dad had the kids two nights a week. We had a statement from one mom who put down that she needed $2,000 a month for clothes and $1,500 a month for hair and makeup and massages. I asked her attorney about the statement in private, and suggested that while she was an entirely presentable woman in appearance, she didn't seem like the type who had a history of being pampered and getting all dolled up. "No," her lawyer said. "She's never been that type. She's been a homemaker. But she thinks she needs to make herself attractive to get a new man." Thankfully, the judge in that case agreed with us: Our client didn't need to finance a Hollywood-style makeover.

One of our lawyers had one of those *Perry Mason* moments in a recent case. The wife filed a statement that said she was working as a waitress at a local restaurant but was earning only $10,000 a year. That's what her tax return said, too. "Hold on," our client said. "Somebody told me she was recently offered a job as the manager of another restaurant in town for $30,000 a year. Why would she turn that down if she was making only $10,000 a year?" That was a very good question. We did a little asking around, and it turned out that the soon-to-be-ex was actually earning more than $30,000 as a waitress, counting the tips she was not reporting to the IRS. When our lawyer got her to admit this in court, the judge not only gave our client very favorable terms for maintenance payments, but also admonished the waitress in no uncertain terms for failing to declare her real income.

One final note about financial statements. They're not carved in stone. A lot can change between January when you first fill out the form and December when your divorce trial finally gets to court. You might get a raise, you might sell some property, you might rent an apartment, you might lease a new car. Keep your lawyer updated on changes in every aspect of your finances—income, expenses, assets, debts—and amend them as appropriate while the divorce is pending, and certainly before you finally get in front of a judge.

DON'T MAKE A STUPID MISTAKE: DO A THOROUGH JOB ON YOUR FINANCIAL RECORDS.

TALKING TOO MUCH— ESPECIALLY TO YOUR WIFE

JAMES WAS A stay-at-home dad, and a good one. Nothing was more important to him than his four-year-old daughter. "Maybe that was one of the problems," he said when he asked us to represent him. "I think my wife thought I paid too much attention to our daughter and not enough to her." James didn't think he could save his marriage—his wife had a boyfriend by then, and had moved in with the other guy—but he wanted things to be as normal as possible for his daughter, including the little girl's relationship with her mother.

When they were still married, James made a habit of giving his wife a detailed rundown every night on their daughter's day. Even if his wife was out of town, he'd tuck the kid in, and then get on the phone and tell his wife about the little girl's triumphs and tribulations throughout the day. James resolved to continue doing that during the divorce, despite the cautions from the lawyer in our firm who represented him. "The less contact the better at this point. Whatever you say will be taken out of context or twisted around by her lawyer to undermine your role as the primary caregiver," our lawyer warned. James insisted that his wife should know everything that was going on with the little girl—for his daughter's sake—and assured us he could be prudent in his remarks.

> *The less contact the better at this point. Whatever you say will be taken out of context or twisted around by her lawyer to undermine your role as the primary caregiver.*

The couple agreed that the little girl would divide her time 50-50 between them during the divorce proceedings, and everything seemed to go smoothly at first. The little girl went to Montessori nursery school class three after-noons a week; sometimes her dad picked her up and sometimes her mom picked her up. One Friday the mom picked up the girl and was supposed to drop her off at the former family home, where James still lived. The little girl came out of the school, all excited, trailing another little girl with her mother.

"They want me to come over and go swimming," the little girl said. "They have a pool in their backyard."

"It'll be fine," the other mother said. "I'll give them a snack, and I'll get in the water with them, and I'll have her home in a couple of hours."

That was very nice, James's soon-to-be-ex said, but their daughter had been suffering from the sniffles for a few days, and it wasn't a good idea for her to go swimming. The other mother said she hadn't realized that, and she understood, and they'd go swimming in a few days when the cold cleared up. The little girl burst into tears and was furious with her mother. Her mom was still trying to calm the little girl down when she dropped her off with James.

"It's probably okay for her to go swimming, but we should be careful," James's soon-to-be-ex told him. "I'm sorry to leave her with you in such a state, but it's your weekend and I'm on my way out of town for the weekend."

"No problem," James told her. "I'll take care of her. I'll call you tonight and check in." James took his daughter into their house, and his wife drove off for the airport.

James hated to see his little girl unhappy. And he thought the cold was almost finished. He called the other little girl's mother to see if the swim playdate offer was still open. James took his daughter over there to swim and picked her up a couple of hours later. That night, as usual, he talked with his soon-to-be-ex and told her everything he knew about the little girl's day in detail—including the swim. James's soon-to-be-ex wasn't pleased that he had overruled her decision to skip the swimming, but she didn't say anything. Not then. Nor did she say anything the following evening when James called her again to tell her about the little girl's day. It hadn't been a good day. Their little girl had awoken with her cold raging again. She had slept most of the day but did not have a fever or other symptoms. The little girl recovered quickly, and she was fine by Monday to go to nursery school.

It was all no big deal, James thought. But his soon-to-be-ex made a major issue of the incident when talking about it the following week with a social worker who had been appointed by the court to do a routine report. The social worker, after questioning James, too, filed a report noting that James had made a "poor parenting choice" that could have seriously harmed his daughter's health, contrary to the mother's more cautious decision. Until then, our firm's lawyer thought James had a good chance of retaining 50-50 custody. The wife's attorney offered a choice: James could accept a custody arrangement that gave him custody about one-third of the time, or the attorney would go to trial and seek to limit James to 20 percent, based on the social worker's negative report. The prospect of a lengthy and expensive custody trial to get that additional time was something James could not afford emotionally or financially. Hoping that his busy soon-to-be-ex-wife would eventually give him additional time during her travels, James took the settlement instead of being guaranteed equal time with his daughter.

James made three mistakes. He let his daughter go swimming. He didn't check with his lawyer first to see if that was a good idea. And he talked too much. He talked himself out of 50-50 custody. Yes, dads going through a divorce need to communicate with their soon-to-be-ex-wives about the kids. But unless the divorce is extremely amicable, most other communication should be through the attorneys to avoid miscommunications and unnecessary discussions.

When you're in litigation, your entire life—everything you say and do—is under a microscope. Sometimes the most innocuous things can end up being used against you. The general rule is this: The less you talk about your divorce, the better—especially to your soon-to-be-ex. This stupid mistake extends beyond merely talking; it also includes texting, e-mailing, leaving out mail or notes, and social networking. (More on that in the next chapter.)

Unfortunately, talking about the breakup is an irresistible impulse for many men. Some men want things to be "normal," or as normal as possible. That's the motivation that hurt James. He wanted to stick to his normal routine of telling his wife everything about their daughter. Well, once somebody files for divorce, normal doesn't exist anymore. Some men want to sit down and eat dinner with their kids and their soon-to-be-exes.

That may or may not be a good idea, depending on the situation, but it's never a good idea if it leads to an after-dinner conversation. It'd be funny if it wasn't sad: Our firm's lawyers expect to get a few calls every Monday morning from chagrined clients who stammer, "Uh, I said something I shouldn't have . . ."

A lot of it, on both sides, is trash talk, pure and simple: My lawyer can beat up your lawyer. I shouldn't have married you in the first place. I never thought you were that great in bed anyway.

When we're frustrated and confused and angry, we lash out with intemperate words.

This is an emotional time. But the divorce proceedings, the legal parts, are no place for emotion. It is difficult, but try to think of it as a business transaction: taking apart the legal contract of the marriage, and unraveling the joint, commingled finances that you shared during the marriage. You need to step back from the emotion, at least in terms of communicating with other people. By continuing to communicate with your soon-to-be-ex, you risk giving away information, making exaggerations, or, worse, making promises as to what you will agree to in resolution of matters, all of which can damage your case. In the heat of an argument, you may make claims you can't back up or the evidence doesn't bear out. Don't assume your statements will go unchallenged. Don't say you have evidence of her cheating, for example, if you don't.

On the flip side, don't attempt to placate the soon-to-be-ex-wife with open-ended promises. One classic example is promising that she can stay in the house until it can be sold and that you will keep paying the mortgage. Sounds fair, but what if the house doesn't sell, she fails to maintain it, she moves the boyfriend in with her, or she moves out? A few months after the divorce, everyone is back in court. Similarly, don't promise to pay for day care, private schooling, the ex-wife's health insurance, or other costs that cannot be pinned down in the future. And never make any promises about custody and visitation.

STICKS AND STONES CAN BACKFIRE

While we're not persuaded that divorced couples need to stay friends, we do know that harsh words during the divorce can lead to long-term hard feelings. Those hard feelings can affect the post-divorce relationship, especially if the ex-husband and ex-wife are sharing responsibility for their kids. They need to be able to communicate effectively and efficiently, and that can be much more difficult if they have said unnecessarily cruel things to each other.

Those hurtful conversations are tempting because they offer short-term gratification. It feels good to unburden yourself, to get your feelings off your chest. You may want to ask your wife why this is happening. You may feel the overwhelming need to express your frustration to her. You may be feeling hurt and alone, and it may seem like talking to friends and family members will make you feel better. Be careful. Assume that everything you say, and everything you write, will be passed along to your soon-to-be-ex and her attorney. Talk to a professional counselor, or your clergy—someone who will not repeat what you say. Talk to your lawyer. We're good listeners. Yes, you should expect to pay your lawyer for this time. But paying your lawyer to listen to you is a bargain in the long run, compared with what it can cost for you to talk to other people for free.

The most destructive conversations typically seem to happen

late at night on Friday or Saturday, usually in the kitchen. Both husband and wife are tired, and maybe one or both has had a drink or two. She says, "I'm going to win."

He says, "No you're not, because my lawyer is going to say you are a bad mother because you took Valium and that you made a mistake on your financial forms. I'm going to get the kids, and I'm going to have to pay you little or nothing."

So what does she do with this new information? The worst-case scenario is that the guy's strategy has worked: He's scared her so much that she thinks she can't win the case and she's never going to get custody, so she grabs the kids and runs. This is a nightmare for everybody, especially the kids, and inevitably leads to a whole new set of legal issues and financial costs.

What happens more often is that she tells her lawyer what she has learned. Her lawyer fixes the mistakes on the financial forms and prepares to show that her doctor prescribed Valium because her husband was driving her crazy. Because of his loose lips, our side gives up the chance to challenge her stability or credibility.

Here's one of our most stark examples, one we pass along to clients all the time. Our client was a successful businessman. He was one of the founders of a small but profitable company that was set up as a limited partnership. His shares were in two different types that had been issued at two different times: half when the company was founded before he and his wife married, and the second half later when the company expanded. His wife wanted half of the total shares. He offered her the half of the shares he got when the company was founded. She agreed, and the case was moving toward a smooth settlement.

What she didn't know was that the company was being re-structured. New investors were coming in. The shares he was keeping would be worth a lot more and the shares she was getting would be worth a lot less. We were scheduled to sign the papers and finalize the divorce when they both showed up at a cocktail party and she started trash-talking.

She mentioned that her lawyer had beaten up our lawyer by getting us to agree to give her the premarital shares and how our client, the "big business guru," had been taken to the cleaners in the divorce. Our client listened for a while, until he couldn't stand it anymore. "Hah," he finally said. "You are so stupid. Wait till you see what you get out of the company, and wait to see what you don't get. Then tell me how smart your lawyer is."

She called her lawyer the next morning and reported the conversation. He began asking questions, and soon learned about the restructuring. Our settlement fell apart. We ended up going to trial several months later, and our client had to give her an additional $1 million because he couldn't keep his mouth shut.

We see this over and over. Whether in anger or jest or a spirit of conciliation, men say, "My lawyer has a plan. This is what we're going to do . . ." And then they lay out our strategy for the case. Don't do that. Don't say anything about the case. To anyone.

This can be difficult when the soon-to-be-ex initiates the conversation. Perhaps she simply wants to know what color you think she should repaint the kitchen, or how she can transform your office into a den once you move out. But maybe she is baiting you, and manipulating you into saying or doing something you shouldn't. We had one client who hated it when his wife told him to calm down. (Actually, most men hate it when their wives tell them to calm down, especially if they are already calm.) This client's wife knew how to push that button, and she used it to her advantage. She'd come over to talk to him; he knew he wasn't supposed to talk to her, but he did. She was being businesslike; it seemed okay to him to talk to her. Gradually, however, she drew him into an argument. At the point he was starting to lose patience with her, she said the magic words: "I wish you would just calm down." He of course exploded at that point, using some very choice words. She was recording it all, which was permissible in the state where they lived, and played it back to her lawyer as an example of his uncontrollable temper.

Even if you and your soon-to-be-ex are entirely civil to each other, don't be tempted to keep communicating. We had another case where our client insisted on contacting his wife almost every day. He'd telephone her, and once in a while stop at her house just to chat. We warned him against this, and told him that her lawyer had also asked us to tell him to stop contacting her so often. But our client's attitude was, "C'mon, it's no big deal. We were together for fifteen years. We can't stop talking to each other just like that." When the case got to court, the woman claimed that he had been harassing her because of all the unwanted contacts, and she had the phone records to back it up. She produced records showing that she had asked her attorney to ask our lawyer to instruct our client to stop contacting her.

Sometimes an estranged wife is so desperate for contact that she will do almost anything to get a response. One example we've seen a number of times is for her to damage some of his stuff—to trash his office or cut up his clothes or put some dents in the 1957 Chevy he's been lovingly restoring for years. Some men will overreact in response. They'll go crazy, screaming and yelling and threatening her, and maybe damaging some of her stuff in return. Don't do it. Be an adult. Call your lawyers and call the cops. Take photos. Take an inventory of what is damaged or missing. Get it on the record.

* * *

LET'S STEP BACK and look at why men talk to their wives, even when their lawyers have advised them against it. There are a number of reasons, most of them emotional. Many men are hurt that they're getting divorced. Their self-image is deflated. They see the divorce as a failure on their part. Someday they will realize that they didn't fail, the marriage failed. But that's a long way off. Many men facing divorce are confused. They have always prided themselves on being in control of their lives, and now their lives are spinning out of control. Some men simply lose control of their emotions and tell their wives about their strategy in the hopes that sharing the strategy or tactics of their case—how strong their case is, in other words—will lead their wives to forget about the divorce and reconcile with them. Some think that spelling out the strength of their case will lead their wives to not fight so hard in court; they think that by showing their cards, the other side will fold and agree to a quick, easy settlement.

Here's the one word that men use to launch so many destructive conversations with their wives:

Why?

Contrary to the popular presumption that men instigate divorce to protect assets or pursue younger women, the typical client we see is a man in his thirties or forties whose wife has decided she wants to end it. Often it's the wife who has the midlife crisis or the seven-year itch or whatever you want to call it. For whatever reason, she wants out. As lawyers, it's not our job to decide who is right or wrong, who is better or worse. Our job is to represent our client as efficiently as possible. And part of that representation is to say, "It's unfortunate, but she may never tell you why she wants a divorce. Or if she does, you may not believe it or understand it. But it doesn't matter. If the marriage cannot be saved, you need to start the process of acceptance, and start moving forward."

And stop talking to her about it. Asking "Why?" is not going to get her back. She has two possible responses. One is to refuse to tell why she wants a divorce. The man can plead, beg, bargain, and ask over and over, but if she isn't going to give a reason, there's nothing he can do about it. He's left feeling even more frustrated and confused, and lacking in control over his own life. She may have no reason, have a reason she doesn't want you to learn, or just want to make you suffer by not knowing.

The other response from the soon-to-be-ex is to give reasons, chapter and verse. Typically, the man refuses to accept the reasons she gives. He argues.

"You're wrong, that is not what happened. Here is what happened . . ." he says.

"No, I'm not wrong," she says. "That is not what happened. You don't know how I feel or what I think."

Arguing isn't going to change her mind. These discussions can get extremely emotional. They can further damage a man's relationship with his wife. If the arguments occur in front of the children, his relationship with the kids can be damaged too. If you can't win an argument, why engage? If the argument is going to do more harm than good, why argue? Things will be said that cannot be taken back. Worse, you may make assertions you have to defend later.

Avoid talking to other people, too, especially family and friends, and in-laws most of all. Many men have the misplaced expectation that they're somehow going to maintain the loyalty of their ex-spouse's family—especially if the wife has had an affair and

she is the one breaking up the marriage. Initially, her family is going to be
disappointed in her, and maybe angry.
They're going to be sympathetic to the

*Avoid talking to other
people, especially family
and friends, and in-laws
most of all.*

wronged husband. "Oh, you poor guy," they say. "We can't believe
she is giving up all you had. We don't understand what's gotten
into her." But that sympathy typically doesn't last long. Family
members will be the man's allies for only a short time. They're
eventually going to rally behind her. After all, they are family.
She is going to rationalize the affair—"He drove me away . . ."
She'll say she's sorry and her family is going to forgive her.

Many men try to maintain good relations with her family
by telling her parents, siblings, and other relatives about how
they intend to move forward based on the strength of their case.
But men need to assume that everything they say to a relative
ultimately will be relayed to the wife, and she will relay it to her
lawyer. Even your own family and friends may share information
with her, either inadvertently or on purpose. For example, we
had a client whose divorce dragged on for six years. It was about
to settle when he got an unexpected inheritance of $300,000.
His soon-to-be-ex would never have known about it, but our client's sister mentioned it to a friend who mentioned it to another
friend who mentioned it to the soon-to-be-ex. The settlement
was scuttled, and our client ended up paying his ex half of the
$300,000.

WHEN SHE SLIPS UP

Occasionally we get a client who wants to play detective; he
wants to talk to his wife either in person or by phone and use a
hidden recorder to get her on tape (or digital recording) saying

The legal issues with recording conversations vary from state to state. Improper recording may create criminal liability, or the conversation may not be admissible in court.

something that we can use in court. We don't ordinarily advise this. For one thing, the legal issues with recording conversations vary from state to state. Improper recording may create criminal liability, or the conversation may not be admissible in court. For another, while most men think they are clever enough to do this, they aren't. They try to lead their soon-to-be-exes into an incriminating conversation, but they are too obvious: "Uh, tell me, honey, I'm just curious, when did you first have sex with your boyfriend in the back of our minivan?" Besides, many men end up getting emotional—either for what she's not saying, or for what she is saying—and start yelling and cursing at her. On tape, of course.

Sometimes a man will act like he wants to get back together with his wife, and he'll say all the right things in order to have her let down her guard and tell him something that he can use against her. We disapprove of this, first because it simply isn't right—it's dishonest—and second because even if she says something incriminating, a judge isn't going to look kindly on our client's deceiving her.

Once in a while, however, a recording can work for us. We have a custody case, as I write this, where the couple keeps having terrible arguments. After one battle, he went home and then called her to apologize. She didn't pick up, so he left a message. She later returned his call, which he let go to his voice mail. "I'm sorry to get so upset," her message said. "I'm just really frustrated that I can't make it without you giving me more money. I can't agree to letting you have the kids more, since that will mean less child support for me. If you'd just pay me more money, I'd give you the kids more." We think that voice mail is going to be extremely damaging to her if we present it as evidence. Basically, she was dangling out more time with the kids in exchange for more money.

We had one client who—on his own, without clearing it with our lawyer first—hid a voice-activated recorder in his wife's car in order to find out if she was having an affair. This backfired for two reasons. First, he found out she was indeed having an affair—with their teenaged daughter's 17-year-old boyfriend. Second, it was a violation of state wiretapping laws that prohibit recording a conversation between two parties when neither has consented. (Surprisingly, that client ended up staying with his wife. We're not sure how he managed this, but he also kept his daughter from finding out about the affair. We wish him luck, but we suspect he'll be coming back to us before long.)

While we're on wiretapping, let's digress into GPS surveillance and snooping into e-mail, phone, bank, and credit card records. Just like wiretapping, hiding a GPS tracker in your wife's car can be illegal. Don't even think about doing it without checking with your lawyer first. Besides, simply knowing where she drove the vehicle is not necessarily proof of anything. Similarly, some guys want to hide a key logger—software that secretly tracks every keystroke on a computer. Check with your lawyer before you do this. If you're already doing it, tell your lawyer immediately.

If phone, bank, credit card, or e-mail records are available for you to see easily, such as on joint accounts, go ahead and look at them. As always, check with your lawyer first, but in general if a mailed statement comes addressed to the two of you and includes records of her phone use or financial activity, make a copy. Similarly, if you have been given access to electronic records by her or have access because they are of a joint account, make printouts.

You may have agreed or allowed her to "take care" of the joint checking account all these years, and now you find she didn't keep the monthly statements. You may be able to get back statements online for months, or even years. One of our clients went into the couple's past joint online banking account statements and learned that she had been sneaking $100 or $200 at a time, once or twice a week, out of their joint account and putting it into an account that was in her name only. Another client found from his credit report that his wife had opened a new credit card account he didn't know about; but it was a joint account since she had used his name and income to qualify. He went online to see her purchases. He made copies of all her statements—and, wisely, never told her. If he had blown up in the middle of an argument and hollered about her opening the account or spending so much money at that new health club and on happy hour drinks, she would have known he had access to the accounts and cut off his access or stopped using the card. Instead, he kept quiet and we had a window on her spending right up to the day of the trial.

We've had a number of clients check their soon-to-be-exes' e-mails, coming and going, throughout the divorce process. They were able to do this, and we were able to use some of the information from the e-mails, because the e-mail account was part of the Internet service in our client's name. The wife neglected to change her password. Not all e-mail accounts can be legally accessed and the laws on access to e-mail accounts are constantly changing, so always check with your lawyer before venturing into her e-mails. Your attorney may be able to obtain the records legally through discovery or subpoena if necessary.

One client brought us a stack of e-mails that his wife had sent to her sister, saying that she had engaged a divorce attorney and was intending to file the papers the following week. We were able to file the next day and gain the advantage of filing first. She was shocked. She had believed she was fooling him, and that he had no idea she wanted a divorce. But seeing her e-mails can backfire. We had one client who was gathering lots of good stuff on his wife from her e-mail but couldn't keep it to himself. He accused her of taking her boyfriend to the restaurant where he had proposed to her eight years earlier. She knew that the only way he could have known that was from her e-mail, so she changed her e-mail.

Because it's so difficult to avoid trash-talking or spilling strategy when talking face-to-face or over the phone, we recommend to many of our clients that they communicate with their wives only through e-mail. That's usually safer, but not always. Use the same brevity and businesslike tone you might use in an e-mail to your boss's boss. Nothing personal. Avoid sarcasm, because that rarely comes across the way you want. Don't use profanity. And don't engage in personal sniping, back and forth. We had one client who responded to his wife's curse-filled, accusatory e-mails by cursing back at her. She saved his e-mails and presented them as evidence of his abusive behavior toward her. He deleted her e-mails and didn't have the same evidence against her. If you're not sure about an e-mail, send it to your lawyer first and ask if it's all right to send it as written.

Here's a final point to take away on the mistake of talking too much about your pending divorce. We urge our clients to look at it from our point of view, as lawyers trying to offer them professional advice and guide them to the best result. When you talk too much, it makes our work—and your case—more complicated, more time-consuming, and more expensive. When we get a call from an opposing attorney saying, "Your client told my client this or that," we have to deal with it. We have to listen and take notes, and then call the client and listen and take notes, and then call back the opposing attorney and try to straighten things out.

Sometimes it's just a misunderstanding; our client doesn't understand what we're trying to do, or how we're trying to do it, and misinforms his soon-to-be-ex. Or perhaps our client understands what we're doing, but the soon-to-be-ex doesn't, and misquotes him to her attorney. If you don't want to be misquoted, don't talk to her. Sometimes we end up back in court if our client has told his soon-to-be-ex something like, "I'm going to take you off my health insurance," or "We've got a plan to make sure you don't get joint custody." It complicates the case. We have to run around trying to put out fires. It's time-consuming, and that means it's expensive—and you as the client have to pay for it.

Another possible complication is the loss of the attorney-client privilege. All communications between a client and his attorney are privileged—which means neither the client nor his attorney can be forced to reveal their communications. However, a client waives that privilege if he tells other people about what was discussed. Suppose you had an arrest for drug possession when you were a teenager—nothing major, but you're not proud of it, and you never told your wife about it. There was no conviction, no one else was involved, and juvenile arrest records in your state are sealed. You need to tell your attorney about it just in case it somehow might come up. You share all the details of the arrest and perhaps other issues that were going on in your life at the time. Under the attorney-client privilege, your lawyer is not obliged to reveal that information to anyone. But if you've told your buddies at the tavern about it, the information may no longer be protected by the privilege. The legal reasoning is that if you want to keep something confidential between you and your lawyer, then don't tell anyone but your lawyer.

Talking to a soon-to-be-ex or anyone else about the case, and particularly the legal strategy, also makes the lawyer wary of how trustworthy the client is. This may be hard to believe, but it is not unusual for a client to get an e-mail from one of our attorneys and then forward it to his soon-to-be-ex. Men seem to do this for the same reasons they talk too much: usually to scare her or make her think we have such a strong case she should settle quickly. It usually backfires the same way. She forwards the e-mail to her attorney, who then knows our strategy and can counter it. When a client gets an e-mail from me and then forwards it to his soon-to-be-ex, I am reluctant to share any more e-mail with that client. I can't fully trust his judgment and his restraint. That hurts our teamwork. We need to be able to trust each other. Remember, you want to be in control. You want to maintain the power in the divorce proceedings. You want to show strength. The real power and the real control and the real strength come from silence.

DON'T MAKE A STUPID MISTAKE: DON'T TALK ABOUT YOUR DIVORCE, ESPECIALLY TO HER.

REVEALING TOO MUCH ON THE INTERNET

ONE OF THE first things we want to know from our clients is how they and their soon-to-be-ex use the Internet. Do they have a Facebook or MySpace page? Do they use Twitter or LinkedIn? Have they signed up for a dating site such as Match.com? Have they posted a video on YouTube? Have they ever gambled online? Do they have a virtual life on Second Life? Do they visit pornography sites?

What you do and where you've been online can say a lot about you as a person. And much of that can be used against you in divorce proceedings. Too many men don't realize how much of their online activity is available to others—or the damage it can cause. Just because you've surfed some X-rated sites and then hit the "delete history" button, that does not mean you've really erased your trail. It may still be there. And just because the photo you posted on Facebook from a party was a night of innocent fun with friends, it can still be used against you and put you on the defensive.

If a client has his own Web page, whether personal or professional, we want to scour it for anything that might be used against him during the divorce. The same with his Facebook or MySpace pages, and for anything he might have posted on Twitter. Too many people don't realize that typing something onto their computer and posting it doesn't mean only their friends will see it. It's out there in public. Anyone can see it, including an estranged wife and her attorney. We've seen many examples of embarrassing social networking posts, but one of the most common is for a guy—or a gal—to create a page and forget to mention the spouse and children. What does that say about honesty and priorities?

Too many men decide that they need to reinvent themselves as they emerge from a failed marriage, and they put forth their new image on Facebook or MySpace. They show themselves on vacation or partying, or make a point of looking for that old high school flame who got away. You don't want to appear in court presenting yourself as a quiet, responsible, churchgoing, sober father—and then have opposing counsel present a MySpace page that shows you playing beer pong or belonging to a Facebook group called "I Hate My Ex-Wife." Remember, everything you put on the Web is the equivalent of gathering your kids, your soon-to-be-ex, her lawyer, social workers, the judge—everyone involved in the case—into the same room and shouting it out loud.

DON'T GET TRAPPED IN THE WORLD WIDE WEB

We urge our clients to edit their social networking profiles on sites such as Facebook and MySpace. We think of these pages as harmless fun, updating our friends on our lives, telling people where we're going and what we're thinking. Social networking can be good, but it can also be bad for marriages—and worse for divorces. Many of the attorneys in our firm advise clients to use social networking only for career building. A few advise against having any sort of page on Facebook or MySpace. You may have tried to protect yourself by making sure your wife and her friends don't know about your Facebook page, or by refusing to "friend" them, but don't be so sure.

The Web is the worst place to keep a secret. And anything can be subject to misinterpretation. You may have put up a

> *The Web is the worst place to keep a secret. And anything can be subject to misinterpretation.*

photo of yourself with the preacher's wife at the annual church potluck picnic; someone else, like a judge, might look at it and ask why is this guy posting a picture of himself with a woman? Anything can be misconstrued.

If a client has a girlfriend, we urge him to take a close look at the girlfriend's postings, too, and give her a little coaching. More than once, we've had a client plead poverty during divorce proceedings, and we learn—and his soon-to-be-ex's attorney learns—via the girlfriend's Facebook or MySpace page that he bought her an expensive piece of jewelry or took her on a luxury vacation. A judge is going to ask, "If this guy doesn't have any money, how can he afford that?" Even worse, the judge could decide that the client is wrongly distributing joint assets from the marriage.

"What can my girlfriend put up on Facebook about me and our relationship?" men ask us.

"Nothing," we respond. "Not a word. Not a single photo. Nothing." However, if the girlfriend is actively posting information on the Internet, she will probably have a hard time editing herself. She will share details about her exciting new relationship.

The information may be all positive, but that will only irritate your ex. Worst case, the girlfriend trash-talks your ex and gives your ex's attorney cause to take her deposition. We have had clients whose girlfriends felt the need to document every incident and issue in the client's divorce; they embellish their secondhand, impassioned accounts and create more problems for our client.

You and your girlfriend may want to alert friends about the big news in your life, but don't do it through a social network posting. Or at least wait until the divorce is final.

We urge our clients to do whatever they can to clean up their "virtual life." Sometimes wives suing for divorce gather evidence beforehand by secretly installing key logger or other software programs that can track every keystroke on a computer. By the time she files, she's accumulated evidence of all the porn and gambling sites he's been visiting. We once had a client whose laptop was subpoenaed by his wife's attorney and turned over to a forensic computer expert who was able to go back and retrace every move—every one—the man had ever made on that laptop.

At the first hint of marital discord, secure your computer. A new password is probably not enough at that point. The cost of anti-spyware software, even the cost of a new computer that you can secure from scratch, is cheap compared with the cost of an incriminating browsing history in terms of financial support, custody arrangements, and litigation expense. Also consider that if your attorney communicates by e-mail, as our clients usually prefer, you don't want your soon-to-be-ex able to get into your computer. Don't go to porn sites or anywhere else that might be embarrassing. Again, the short-term limitations on your Internet use are a small price compared to the cost of extended litigation over your online conduct.

Some lawyers have started asking for user names and

passwords during the discovery process: They want to see what the other side has been putting up on Facebook and MySpace. We don't routinely do that, mostly because it makes the wife run straight to the computer and start erasing things or causes allegations later by the opposing party as to who accessed or changed the website. We prefer to obtain the information indirectly if possible, or under oath from the opposing party if necessary. But it's good for men facing divorce to remember that the court can order them to turn over their user names and passwords. It's often difficult and costly, but the experts can and do retrieve chats and instant messages that otherwise seem to simply disappear into space. Tell your lawyer about all your Internet habits or postings at the outset. And even if there's no smoking gun, we've been able to persuade judges that a mom can't be doing the very best job possible with her kids if she is spending five or six hours a day glued to Facebook. She's literally stealing time from the kids. If the same argument can be lodged against you, your lawyer needs to know.

While we check out our client on the Web, we check out their soon-to-be-ex, too. It's amazing what people will put out there. If a wife posts on her Facebook wall, "I kicked him out and took the kids and cleaned out the bank accounts," she's going to have a difficult time portraying herself as a victim in court. More than once we've found that wives have listed themselves as single, no kids, and looking for dates—even while they were still married and have kids. There's nothing illegal about most of the stuff people make up about themselves on the Web, but at the very least it makes them look dishonest. And judges don't like dishonesty.

Sometimes you have to do a little sleuthing to find the wife's digital trail. Some women use their middle names, maiden names, or other nicknames for their online personas. Some use code words or names when communicating to other men, thinking the rest of the world is stupid and can't figure it out. We'll ask the question, "Uh, ma'am, can you tell us, please, why you address this certain man online as 'Mr. Big Johnson?' What exactly does that mean, ma'am?" At about that moment she is turning red and her attorney is looking for a table to crawl under. We don't ordinarily recommend this—check with your lawyer if you're tempted to try it—but one of our clients joined Facebook under an assumed name and "friended" his soon-to-be-ex. She turned out to be more than happy to chat with strangers—and to send them photos of herself. At first the photos were just normal snapshots, but with our client's encouragement she was soon sending not only nude shots of herself, but also videos, including one that could only be described as pornography. Yes, she settled on the advice of her attorney.

If she's on Facebook or MySpace, we urge the client to print it out, noting the date, time, and website address information—every page, in color, please—as soon as possible, because her attorney is probably telling her to clean up her presence on the Web, too. In general, it is illegal to use her password and check her accounts; under the law, she has a fair expectation of privacy. But check with your lawyer. If the two of you have a common family account, or you (or a mutual friend who is willing to assist) have been given access to her accounts previously, your lawyer might decide you can legitimately obtain the printouts of her information.

We're going to use examples from Facebook, since that's probably the most popular social networking site, but the lessons and advice pertain to other sites, too. If your wife never "friended" you or has recently "de-friended" you, find someone else who is friends with her, and look over that person's shoulder and then print out her pages. Many dads are able to monitor their kids' online activity, which may include the kids going to their mom's page, since moms often friend their kids. Or maybe some of her real-life friends are also her Facebook friends and will help you. Once you have the pages printed out, if there is anything that might be objectionable, discuss with your attorney about whether to address it. If she has a photo up of herself in a revealing swimsuit or with a new guy, your attorney may advise you to send her a note—or your attorney may e-mail her attorney—documenting that this is inappropriate. It doesn't need to be anything that might get her sent to jail; it just needs to be something that allows you to say, "You know, I don't think our kids should see this. It doesn't send them the right message about you . . ."

Common mistakes on Facebook—for both men and women—are to go searching for old high school girlfriends and boyfriends, friending them and then chatting with them and maybe flirting with them. From an evidence standpoint, a post doesn't need to be proof of cheating. It doesn't need to say, "Wow, I enjoyed having sex with you last night." Merely showing interest can be damaging, too, especially if your case is in front of a judge who takes a strict view of infidelity. Technically, of course, the husband and wife are still married during the divorce proceedings. They do not become the ex-husband and the ex-wife until the final divorce decree is granted. In the real world, of course, most judges won't be such sticklers. If a man starts dating several months into a contested divorce, most judges won't hold it against him. But we've done very well in a number of past cases when we've learned that a wife was looking for boyfriends—going on Match. com or listing herself as single on Facebook—even before she mentioned to her husband that she might want to split up. We assure our clients that we are not making moral judgments about them. But the image they present to the rest of the world can be very important. Okay, you met someone, you went for coffee, you took her to dinner and a movie, and you'd like to see her again. That's fine. But why put it on Facebook and blab to the whole world about it? What do you have to gain by broadcasting it? We know what you have to lose—your money and your time with your kids. Is it worth the risk?

USING THE WEB TO YOUR ADVANTAGE

Our lawyers have found some amazing things posted by the soon-to-be-ex-wives of our clients. One woman put a post on Facebook about going to a party, throwing up, not remembering how she got home, and then not being able to get out of bed until two o'clock the next afternoon. No, that did not help her custody case. Another woman bragged on MySpace about how she was going to court to try to get our client to pay more child support. "I'm going to get paid today," she wrote. The judge did not look kindly on her view of child support as a personal pay-day. A third had posted her cathartic musings about how leaving her family was the best thing she had done and that her children were better off with their father; that made our client's motion to move the children to another state much less complicated.

One woman who had some issues with alcohol was ordered by the court to give up drinking and attend Alcoholics Anonymous meetings regularly. The social worker on the case told her that was the only way the judge was going to allow her joint custody of the kids. Lo and behold, she posts pictures on Facebook of a party. Not only is she holding up a can of Bud Light, and not only are there empty shot glasses lined up in front of her, but in the background of the picture you can see her kids. She had blocked our client from seeing the account, but one of her friends was so concerned about the mom's behavior and her ability to be a good mother that the friend printed out the page and gave it to our man.

In each of these cases, the evidence was persuasive—so persuasive that we didn't even need to present it in court. Our lawyers showed it to their lawyers, who variously rolled their eyes, slapped their foreheads, uttered expletives, and said, "Okay, let's settle this case. What do you want?" Online evidence like this typically causes so much embarrassment that it rarely makes it into court. Instead, it is persuasive in gaining a favorable settlement. Opposing attorneys know how risky it is to fight such evidence.

Now, that does not mean that incriminating evidence from the Web is a slam dunk. As Internet law evolves, we're seeing a whole body of cases develop around the issue of electronic discovery—what sort of evidence from the Web can be introduced in court. Some attorneys try to prevent the court from hearing evidence from social networking sites by arguing that it is hearsay and that there is no way to substantiate the content. It depends on the jurisdiction, sometimes from judge to judge, but in general, website evidence is going to be admissible if it is produced as a printout of an actual Web page.

But even if evidence from the Web might not be admissible in court, that doesn't mean it isn't valuable. The mere fact that we know there is a boyfriend can send us off looking for him or other witnesses to confirm it. We might end up with better evidence in the form of eyewitnesses.

Here's how we've seen it play out a number of times: We see something online that makes us think the wife may be cheating. There's no proof, but she is flirting in words and pictures, and maybe presenting an image of herself as a playgirl. We can't prove it. And maybe our evidence isn't even admissible. No problem. We can go to the other side, to the woman and her attorney, and say, "Okay, we're not interested in presenting this Web page as evidence in court. But we do want to talk to the people who are in the picture with her, so we need the names and addresses of everyone in the picture as potential witnesses. We know she has been chatting back and forth online with a guy named John Smith. We'd like to question Mr. Smith. And we're going to question Mrs. Smith too." In the face of subpoenas flying all through her social life, the wife is suddenly more agreeable to settlement.

In some ways, the worst examples are when the wife posts inappropriate things that the kids can see. She wants to be friends on Facebook with her kids; who doesn't? But she also wants to start her new life of fun. In one custody contest, the 46-year-old housewife apparently had a boyfriend. The boyfriend would make up songs and post them on YouTube—little love songs to his new girlfriend. Pretty soon she was doing the same thing, making up little love songs to her new boyfriend and posting them on YouTube. They never mentioned each other by name, but it was clear from the lyrics that the two people were aiming the songs at each other—how exciting it was to start a new relationship, and so on. Our client, also in his forties, saw the videos and was horrified. This estranged mom's new boyfriend was a 21-year-old guy who worked for the lawn service that cut the grass at the couple's house. Even worse, the mother had allowed the couple's ten-year-old daughter, who recognized the man as the "lawn boy," to see the videos—both the boyfriend's and her mom's—and the ten-year-old had shown them to her little brothers, ages eight and six.

Our client was not happy, and neither was the judge. He

called the wife in and said, "Cut it out." She decided to give the judge some attitude. "Your Honor, I am no longer married," she said. "We are separated. I am allowed to date." The judge, fuming, didn't explicitly tell her to dump the boyfriend, but it was clear that this was one of those judges who thinks that you're married until the divorce decree is final, and any fooling around before that is adultery. "Dating, as you call it, may be your business, but broadcasting your behavior for your children to see is inappropriate and unacceptable," the judge said. "I don't want to hear about any more of this." This happened in Georgia, one of the states where evidence of adultery can mean giving up alimony, so the wife ended up settling out of court without the fight our side had been expecting.

Dating may be your business, but broadcasting your behavior for your children to see is inappropriate and unacceptable.

Even if the mom is not posting videos of herself pole-dancing, we can score points for the dad if she includes the kids on her Facebook page at all. We've had a number of cases where the mom has simply put up too much information about her kids— their names, ages, photos, where they go to school, their after-school activities, and more. In this day and age, that's not being a responsible parent or doing your best to protect your kids. Such postings about the kids also usually neglect to mention the father, or may imply our client is out of the picture. Comments such as the mother "had" to take care of a sick child or "had" to find a babysitter to watch the kids while she went out on a date can be used to show her attempts to alienate the client from his children by not informing him of their illness or to cross-check the dates when she told the client she was home with the kids so he couldn't see them, when apparently she had turned the kids over to a third party instead of their father.

One of our attorneys used Facebook to find a wife who had run off with our client's kids. Our client was trying to serve her with legal documents—the petition for divorce, along with orders for her to return the kids to him—and she was ducking the process server. She was apparently staying with friends, moving from one house to another, and every time our process server went to one of the houses, he was told that she had moved on. Nobody ever knew where she had gone. But our client was hearing from people who had seen her, so we knew she was still in the area. Our lawyer checked Facebook and noted that she had agreed to meet a certain friend at a certain time at a certain restaurant. Our process server was there, too, and delivered the legal papers that set the divorce in motion and forced her to return the kids.

BEYOND FACEBOOK AND MySpace, we've seen people get into financial trouble by gambling online. In one case, the soon-to-be-ex-wife thought she had covered her tracks, but we were able to trace her credit card payments through PayPal and make a convincing case to the judge that she had been dissipating marital assets through her gambling losses.

One of our lawyers also had an interesting case where the soon-to-be-ex-wife was playing the virtual reality game Second Life, where you create and control an avatar, a digital person who "lives" in the virtual world. Our client discovered that his wife had established a presence in Second Life with an avatar that was remarkably like her—except the image was a little younger and sexier, of course. She had set up a virtual family that mirrored their real-life family—husband who worked as a banker and wife who had a law degree but stayed home with their eleven-year-old daughter and five-year-old son. All that was fine, but our client was shocked to learn that his wife's avatar had divorced her husband in Second Life, and was having all sorts of virtual affairs with other avatars. There was nothing illegal about this, of course—it's just a game, her attorney said—but it gave the judge reason to wonder what was going on in the wife's "real" world.

DON'T MAKE A STUPID MISTAKE:
BE CAREFUL ABOUT ANYTHING
YOU PUT ON THE INTERNET.

FAILING TO
FULLY ENGAGE
IN YOUR CASE

PRESTON WAS ANGRY. He was angry at his estranged wife, at her lawyer, and at me, his lawyer. Opposing counsel had served a subpoena upon his employer, ordering the production of his employment records. He had been embarrassed that a process server brought the subpoena to his workplace, in front of his co-workers. Several hours later, at home, Preston was still seething when he called me.

"What is this bull [expletive deleted]?" Preston demanded. "I thought you were supposed to take care of all this for me. You're my lawyer. Why am I paying you if you're not going to take care of this [expletive deleted, same one]?"

I let him blow off steam, and more expletives. Then I said, gently but firmly, "Preston, this happened because you have not been participating in your case as much as you could or should. My office has told you several times that we needed your financial information, and the other side would need it, too. We e-mailed you the forms to fill out. When we didn't get them back right away, we sent the forms to your house by snail mail. When we still didn't hear anything, our legal assistants called you several times and left messages. We explained that this was important and had to be taken care of. You blew us off and you're blowing off your case. I'm afraid you can expect your banks and creditors will also be served with subpoenas."

That was not what Preston wanted to hear. He wanted to be angry. He didn't say much, so I pressed him. "Preston, why did you ignore us? Didn't you get the e-mails?"

"I got 'em," he mumbled. "I just didn't read 'em. All that bull [expletive deleted, you know which one] is just bad news, just a hassle. I didn't want to deal with it. I thought you would take care of everything for me."

No. That's a common misconception. Lawyers do not take care of everything in a divorce case. Too many men do not get as involved in their own cases as they should. They don't en-gage. This is the client's case, and he's the one making the allegations and putting his case forth. Clients need to understand this: The lawyer is an advisor and advocate who can only work with the information provided and argues the law based upon that information; the client needs to supply the informa-tion, the evidence. Without the evidence, the lawyer cannot argue the application of the law. Too many clients regard them-selves as bystanders, watching the divorce unfold.

Lawyers do not take care of everything in a divorce case. Too many men don't get as involved in their own case as they should.

Perhaps this misconception is drawn from depictions of legal proceedings in television or movies. Clients in these shows always seem to be clueless as to what is happening to them until the lawyer explains everything at the climax. Unfortunately, divorces don't play out that way. You have already written the "script" to your marriage (and now the divorce), and we need you to explain it to us.

Another possible explanation for this expectation is that the client may have been involved in other legal proceedings, perhaps a personal-injury case. In many other types of litigation, the client does "drop off" the case with the law firm, which then assembles police reports, deposes doctors, and negotiates settlement with the other side, usually an insurance company.

If you are willing to accept whatever the other side (your soon-to-be-ex) is willing to offer in settlement, then perhaps your case can be handled without your involvement. Many "flat-rate" divorce attorneys in fact approach cases in this manner. We have found that waiting to accept the "usual deal" from the other side never serves our clients well, which is why we always proceed on the assumption that a trial will be required and why we prepare accordingly. And in order to prepare for possible trial, you, the client, need to be fully involved in your case: the captain of the ship, while the lawyer serves as the harbor pilot. We touched on this earlier, in Chapter 2, during the discussion of how to choose the right lawyer. Now we want to look in more detail about exactly what the client's role should be not only in helping the lawyer build the case, but in pushing and sometimes challenging the lawyer to do his or her best work.

HOW MUCH IS ENOUGH?

Male divorce clients generally can be divided into two types: those we never hear from—they're "off the grid," we joke in our office—and those who contact us all the time. Sometimes it can be exasperating to hear from clients every day when they call or e-mail to tell us everything that happens, and every thought that crosses their minds—everything from their six-year-old losing her first tooth to suspecting that their soon-to-be-ex is planning to move out of state. Contacting us every day also means they have to pay us to respond every day. Even if it's only a ten-minute conversation or e-mail exchange, a lawyer who charges $300 an hour has to charge the client $50 for that. We urge clients to save up all the little status items that don't require legal advice and reach out to us once a week. We need to be kept informed as to what is going on in your life and family to best advise you, but we also advise that you "don't sweat the small stuff." That said, we much prefer the client who is in constant contact to the ones who go off the grid. Literally, we can work with them.

Too many men get in touch only if there's a crisis. That's why my attorneys and I keep our cell phones on over the weekend and in the evenings—when a crisis is most likely to happen. On weekdays, most people are at work and most kids are at school. It's during the time off, on evenings and weekends, that the arguments occur and the threats are made and someone violates the terms of the custody agreement. It's not unusual for us to get a call from an upset client who says, "I haven't seen my kid in three weeks, and you're not doing anything about it." More often than not, we say, "Well, the last we spoke was several weeks ago. Have you read and signed the statement we sent you after that last incident, which we need to attach to your pleadings to get a court date? You haven't kept us informed as to the details of what is going on. We need you to update the specifics—the times when your wife refused to let you see your son—before we can go back to the court and take care of this."

Many of our clients are tardy in contacting us because they simply don't want to get divorced, or at least they don't want to face the reality of being divorced and take care of the details involved in the divorce proceedings. It's painful to pull the evidence together, and for many men it's painful to talk about the divorce, even to their lawyers. I think that's a big reason so many clients want us to contact them primarily via e-mail instead of phone or office conferences these days, and that's fine with us—as long as they check their e-mails and respond promptly. If we request information or a position on an issue, don't ignore the request, no matter how much you don't want to do it. At least confirm that you received the e-mail, and give us an idea of how long it will take you to answer our questions or provide the documents we need. Give yourself a deadline, plot out some time to gather the evidence or fill out the forms, and stick to it.

The most difficult clients for us to work with are the ones who don't care about the details and won't pay the necessary attention to the case to help themselves. They also seem to be the ones who are most likely to blame their lawyers if they don't get the result they like. A good example is the guy who has lived his entire life ignoring the details. "I don't sweat the small stuff," this kind of guy told us. He may be an intelligent man, but he probably doesn't have as good a job as he might. Maybe he never applied himself in school, and he has never been particularly ambitious or detail-oriented. He might always remember to get a hunting license, but he might "forget" to renew his driver's license or vehicle registration. He hates deadlines and details, and he's lived his entire life that way. In fact, that might be part of the reason he's getting divorced. He never paid enough attention to his wife, or put enough hard work into the marriage. He didn't listen to his wife, and he doesn't listen to his lawyer.

Don't be that guy. And even if you've been that guy in the past, don't be that guy now, during your divorce. It's time for a fresh start. This is an opportune time to get organized, to start meeting deadlines, and to start assuming responsibility for every aspect of your life.

If you have been that guy, your lawyer's office should help you get organized and meet deadlines for your divorce. It may cost you a few bucks to turn over your boxes or piles of unorganized financial documents for a legal assistant to organize and identify missing documents, but without complete, organized documents your lawyer cannot navigate your case to its optimum conclusion. Your lawyer should provide you regular updates by letter or e-mail, reminding you of the deadlines and decision points in your case. We provide status letters or e-mails biweekly in order to keep the clients current on the constantly changing status of their case and court dates. Again, this may cost you a few dollars, but missing a court date or compliance deadline can be much, much more costly.

Let's pinpoint some of the ways that clients need to be particularly involved and proactive. For one, you need to be fully cooperative during the entire discovery process and alert to information that might help your lawyer further the case. You need to engage your lawyer as to the legal tactics and issues; ask whether the assigned judge presents any particular challenges or how you might obtain favorable temporary orders. If the temporary orders are disadvantageous, you need to push your lawyer to get a quick trial date to receive a more reasonable final judgment. Finally, if a lawyer isn't doing a good job, the client needs to be prepared to fire that lawyer and find a new one.

Discovery is the process during which each side gathers its evidence. Much of that evidence, such as the financial statements, must be shared with the other side. Each side also can present interrogatories—questions that the other side ordinarily must answer. Like financial statements, the answers to interrogatories are considered sworn statements under oath. You can have a huge influence on the case by providing your lawyer with information—and suspicions—that help your lawyer formulate the interrogatories.

The goal is to seek and gather answers to the interrogatories that can help buttress your position. For example, if you suspect that your wife is in the process of renting a house near her mother in the next state, we want to ask about that. If you suspect that your wife might have spent money from your joint assets without telling you, we want to ask about that. Generally, lawyers are limited in the amount of discovery that can be demanded from the other side, to avoid the parties from attempting to overwhelm the other side with frivolous requests. Therefore, your lawyer needs to focus the discovery requests to target the critical issues that need exploration. Your lawyer can't fine-tune the attack without your "intelligence" on what your soon-to-be-ex may have done or will accuse you of doing.

It's a classic example of the client becoming an active participant in the case, instead of simply leaving everything to the lawyer. If you like the war analogy for divorce, this is where you gather your weapons and muster your troops. The facts are your weapons, and your troops—your lawyer and your law firm—need those weapons to formulate a legal strategy for your case.

> *The facts are your weapons, and your troops—your lawyer and your law firm—need those weapons to formulate a legal strategy for your case.*

Discovery is not a one-way street, of course. The other side gets to present interrogatories to us, too. It's the client's responsibility, not the lawyer's, to answer the questions honestly. "Just take care of that for me and I'll sign it," some clients say. We're not going to do that. The information must come directly from the client. We're happy to advise on how—or whether—to answer certain questions, but it is up to the client to do a first draft, to answer the questions the best he can. You're not alone in this. It's a team effort. You'll talk to, and maybe sit down with, lawyers and legal assistants to explain the "legalese" in the questions, how the answers impact your case, and work on your answers. We'll go over the answers, clean up the phrasing, and edit the scope of the response—we're not required to go beyond the narrow scope of the question—but in the end the client has to read the answers, agree that they are accurate, and sign a statement swearing that the answers are true.

If a client is going to learn about the legal aspects of divorce, that usually happens during the discovery process. Most men don't want to know any more than necessary. A few men want us to basically give them private law school tutoring. As lawyers, we're happy to explain what we think the client needs to know about the process and why the facts are important, but at some point the tutoring can become counterproductive. It can cost the client more than it's worth. At that point, let the lawyer handle the legal aspects. If you've got new information, more facts that might help the lawyer, speak up.

Earlier, during a discussion of the advantages of filing first for divorce (Chapter 3), we touched on how the terms of the temporary orders are issued by the court soon after the divorce papers have been filed. These temporary orders set the framework for financial support payments and the terms of child custody and visitation during the months of the divorce process. Suppose that under the court's temporary orders the man has been paying more than he thinks he should for child support and maintenance. His soon-to-be-ex has residential custody of the kids and he gets to see the kids less than he'd like. But he's kept his mouth shut. He hasn't rocked the boat. He's scraped and scrimped and cut back on his own lifestyle in order to make the payments. He's made the best of his limited time with the kids, even though he'd love to have 50-50 joint custody. Then it comes time for the trial, and the judge looks at the temporary orders and says, "Why should we change anything? This seems to be working. Nobody is complaining. Let's stick with what is in place and make it permanent." The man and his lawyer never should have settled for the bad temporary orders. By not complaining or objecting when they had the chance, they rolled over for the wife and her attorney. This is one of those instances where the squeaky wheel gets the grease.

When preparing for the hearing to determine temporary orders—the financial payments and custody arrangement that will be in place during the divorce proceedings, before the final decree—some clients do not push hard enough for what they want. And some lawyers don't push hard enough on their clients' behalf. If you can't afford to pay more than a certain amount per month, say so and provide your lawyer the financial records in support of your position. If you want more time with your kids than your soon-to-be-ex is offering, speak up and give your lawyer the specifics and list of potential witnesses to your parenting skills. If your lawyer tells you not to worry, that it's only temporary, or tells you that it's a big hassle to object to what she is offering, you should listen to your lawyer—but you can also question your lawyer. What else can the lawyer do? Maybe it's worth the hassle to you. Maybe you want to object to the temporary orders anyway. Don't be afraid to be pushy with your lawyer. When clients, or their lawyers, don't fight hard enough for favorable temporary orders, the client may suffer for it for years afterward.

This is not to say you have to slavishly follow your attorney's advice regarding temporary orders. We welcome healthy skepticism and arguments, and we want clients to follow their own heads—and hearts—even if it means ignoring our advice. But if a client does decide to challenge the temporary orders against our advice, we want to make sure he has been fully engaged. We want to make sure he understands our strategy, and the basis for our advice. We want to make sure he understands the risks and consequences. Listen to your attorney, and ask questions if you don't understand anything.

Listen to your attorney, and ask questions if you don't understand anything.

We often see this early in a case, and often when custody is an issue. A dad will come in and say he doesn't want to push for custody in the temporary orders because he wants the process to be civilized and not contentious. He says he and his wife are getting along, and she would never deny him access to the kids. But if it isn't on paper, if it isn't part of a court order, that's exactly what happens: They don't get along as well as he would like, and he doesn't get to see the kids as much as he would like.

We had a recent case brought to us by a man named William. His wife's attorney proposed that she have residential custody of their two boys, a toddler and an infant, during the divorce proceedings. There was no provision for William to have the kids overnight, ever. We said he should insist on getting the boys at least one weekend a month, in addition to seeing them during the day at least once a week. "No need for that," William told us. "There are a lot of problems with my wife, but she's always really encouraged me to be involved with the babies. She'll give me more time whenever I want it." He and his wife were parting as friends, he said, and they were getting along well. It was going to be an amicable divorce. He ignored our advice and signed the temporary orders.

Things changed rapidly, of course. William's soon-to-be-ex found a new friend who was a member of a local motorcycle club that didn't have the best reputation. They didn't seem to be mixed up in any major crimes, but they were known for their tricked-out Harleys, ponytails, tattoos, and bar fights. The mom began spending more and more time with this biker, and with his biker buddies. She left the kids most of the time with her mother, who was retired and who loved the kids and was happy for them to basically move in with her. Whenever William wanted the kids, his wife had some excuse. Before long she was simply ignoring his calls. When William tried to call the grandmother, she'd hang up on him. A couple of times he showed up at Grandma's house, hoping to see the kids, but she told him to go away or she'd call the cops. William didn't want any trouble, so he left.

Over the course of eleven months before we got to trial, William saw his boys twice, only for a couple of hours each time. His soon-to-be-ex never let him have them overnight. Meanwhile, he began hearing things about her smoking a lot of pot. He decided the little boys would be better off with him, and asked us about his chances when the divorce case went to trial. He was hoping the judge would award him primary custody. We said we would try it, but the odds were again him because he had seen so little of the kids. At trial, we were able to raise enough questions about the mother's behavior that it was clear the kids should not be with her. Meanwhile, however, her lawyer pointed out that William had barely seen the kids over all those months; he didn't seem like he was going to win any awards for parenting, either. The judge wasn't buying William's explanation that he would have seen the boys more if their mother and grandmother had allowed it. The judge seemed to take the attitude that if William had really wanted his kids, he would have done more to show that he wanted them, such as litigating the temporary orders. Fair or not, judges consider the failure to take advantage of litigation opportunities as a lack of interest in the issue, even if the reasons for not litigating may have been well-intentioned. The judge awarded primary custody not to either parent, but to the grandma.

William made another mistake in the early stages of that case by not allowing us to push for a quick trial date. He never said so specifically, but my guess is that he was secretly hoping to reconcile with his wife, and he reckoned that as long as he put off making it official, there was still a chance of getting back together. That worked against him in conjunction with the unfavorable temporary custody orders. If a judge issues temporary orders that we view as unfavorable to our client, we want to push for a quick trial date. If our client is paying more than we think he should, or if he is not seeing the kids as much as we think he should, we need to get back in front of the judge for a final decision as soon as possible. The longer the temporary orders are in effect, the more everybody gets used to them, the more they become the norm, and the more likely the judge at trial is to say, "Well, it's been working all this time, why should we change anything?" When a judge first issues temporary orders we don't like, we'll immediately request a quick trial date. Sometimes we'll indicate that we might challenge the temporary orders unless we get the quick trial date, and most judges don't want to have to hold yet another hearing. Consequently, many judges will set a quick trial date as a sort of accommodation. I'm convinced that if we had been able to get William to trial in two or three months instead of eight months, it would have been easier for him to show that he really wanted the kids. He would have been trying to get them back as quickly as possible, instead of letting the case go on for nearly a year while they got settled in with Grandma.

Mark is another client who failed to take to heart the need to step up and participate in his case. Mark also hoped to reconcile with his wife and refused to accept that divorce was inevitable. Mark came to us at the outset of his case and we laid out the possible issues and strategies based upon the information he provided. Mark said he would think about it and get back to us. Three months later he was back. His wife's attorney had set a court date on temporary orders, which Mark failed to attend. He hadn't paid attention to the letters from her attorney and the court, assuming his wife would not really proceed with the case. Now he was out of the house with no set schedule with his kids. We reviewed the issues and advised him to file for reconsideration of the temporary orders. Again he begged off. He was sure his wife would not proceed with the divorce.

In fact, she did let him back in the house for a while, so she could finish her employment training, and then kicked him out when she no longer needed him to watch the kids. We then obtained a prompt court date and prepared for trial. We were able to present Mark with a reasonable settlement option; he balked, but eventually agreed to the settlement, hoping that doing so would curry favor with his now ex-wife. Several months later Mark called again. The ex-wife had filed for a protective order against him because he kept calling her and showing up at her door and asking her if they could try to get back together. Mark's refusal to accept the reality of the divorce, pay attention to the proceedings, or listen to our advice has left him frustrated and mistakenly blaming "the system" for his situation, much of which could have been avoided had he been proactive in addressing the issues in his case.

Conversely, if we like the temporary orders and our client would be happy to live long and prosper under them, we're not as eager to push for a quick trial date. Sure, our client still wants the divorce to be over and done with, the sooner the better in most cases. But the longer the favorable temporary orders are in effect, the more of a track record as to what our client's post-divorce conduct and finances will look like, and the more likely the terms of the financial support and custody are to become permanent in the final divorce decree, whether at trial or in a settlement.

It may be heresy for a lawyer to bring this up, but we also should consider what happens if you think your attorney is mis-handling your case. When do you fire your lawyer and bring in a new one? It happens surprisingly often, or maybe it seems that way simply because our firm gets so many clients who come to us because they have been unhappy with their first attorneys. Let me give you some thoughts from the perspective of a lawyer who is often brought into a case that a client believes is going wrong. We've covered (Chapter 2) many of the mistakes that lawyers make and what you should look for when you're choosing a law-yer. But now let's discuss what to do when the case is under way and you're dissatisfied.

The key is whether you—and your case—will fare better with a new lawyer. Even if your first lawyer has made some mis-steps that you think another lawyer might not have made, it may not be worth it to make a change. For one thing, you need to consider how it looks to the judge. Most judges understand that sometimes a client and a lawyer are not a good working team. To them, it's no big deal if a client gets a new lawyer. But to some judges, changing lawyers is the sign of a troubled or trouble-some client. After all, every judge was a lawyer before becoming a judge, and knows what it is like to deal with clients. If a judge has seen you change lawyers once, don't contemplate doing it again—that would be a sure sign to many judges that you are a difficult client.

If you are thinking of changing lawyers, don't fire your first lawyer until you have retained the new one. Go through all the same steps we discussed earlier for finding a new lawyer, including interviewing one or more attorneys. Perhaps you'll want to go back to one or more of the lawyers you interviewed previously. Ask these lawyers about the wisdom of switching horses midstream. Bring in the details of what has happened in your case and how things are going with the judge. A good lawyer may well advise you to stick with your current lawyer until a certain point in the case; at that point, depending on what happens, the lawyer may advise a change—or not.

One final caution, not only when thinking about changing lawyers, but to remember in all your dealings with your lawyer: Even if an attorney does the best job possible and gives you the best representation possible, you may not—you probably will not—get all the results you want. You want a lawyer who is always prepared and communicating with you. You want to be part of a team, and it's up to you, just as much as your lawyer, to make sure the team works smoothly.

DON'T MAKE A STUPID MISTAKE:
BE FULLY ENGAGED IN YOUR CASE
WITH YOUR LAWYER.

BEING ILL-PREPARED FOR TESTIMONY AND INTERVIEWS

RAYMOND, THE MANAGER of an Olive Garden restaurant, came to us the day after his wife said she wanted a divorce. In the months since then, he had been a model client. He had done everything our lawyer asked him to do. He had been fully engaged in his case and worked with our lawyer to prepare it. In the weeks just prior to trial, he had spent several hours going over documents in the case file and talking with his lawyer, one of my colleagues, about what was going to happen in court when he took the stand in his trial.

First he would testify under direct examination, answering questions about the issues he and his lawyer had identified as being important to his case. Then he would be cross-examined, probably in much less friendly tones, by his soon-to-be-ex-wife's lawyer. If we needed to clarify anything that opposing counsel brought up, our lawyer would have the chance to ask follow-up questions in redirect.

We tried to prepare Raymond for the unexpected. The judge could interrupt with questions. The lawyers could object to questions, and object to Raymond's answers. If there were objections raised during his testimony, Raymond should not speak until the lawyers and judge resolved the issue. Above all, we emphasized the need for Raymond to listen to the questions carefully. He needed to make sure he clearly understood the question, and then answer the question that was asked without attempting to fill in any additional information that wasn't requested.

When the trial date came and Raymond took the stand, things started off well with the direct examination. Raymond was exactly what lawyers want in a witness. He was a little nervous, even though he was trying to act relaxed. But that's normal for anybody who's taking the stand in a courtroom for the first time. He answered the questions calmly and to the point. He recapped the details of the agreements he and his soon-to-be-ex had made over splitting up their property. He accurately and fully described his financial situation. He testified about his relationship with his children, that he wanted joint custody, and how the children would split their time 50-50 between his ex-wife's house and his house. Much of the financial and property information was set forth in documents, which kept his direct testimony time down to a little over an hour and a half.

Our lawyer thanked Raymond and sat down. The soon-to-be-ex-wife's lawyer took over for cross-examination. The opposing lawyer ran through the financial and property testimony, trying to challenge Raymond on his numbers, but Raymond was solid on his financial facts and handled that part of the cross-examination without a problem. Then opposing counsel asked about Raymond's job at the Olive Garden: Did he sometimes get irritated with customers who were inconsiderate to the staff or other diners? Raymond, his brow furrowed, answered yes, once in a while he had to deal with annoying customers. Raymond clearly did not know where this was going. He was beginning to feel confused. What did this have to do with his divorce?

"Do you ever feel like lashing out at those annoying people?" the opposing attorney asked him.

"Uh, well . . ." Raymond was about to answer. Our attorney tensed ever so slightly. Would Raymond blurt out some flippant answer, like saying sometimes he wished he could stick a fork in the backsides of annoying customers? Our lawyer leaned forward. Any inappropriate comment, even said in jest, could derail a promising case.

Instead of answering immediately, Raymond paused. He took a few seconds. He took a deep breath. And then he said, "No."

"You don't have a violent temper?" the lawyer asked.

Again, Raymond paused a few seconds and said no.

"Do you hit your children?" the lawyer asked.

Raymond paused to consider this extremely loaded question, and as he frowned in thought, our lawyer objected to the question as improperly assuming that the children had ever been hit by either parent, as there had not been any evidence of such up to that point in the trial.

"I'll rephrase. Have you *ever* hit any of your children?" the lawyer asked.

"Yes," Raymond said.

Later, on redirect, our lawyer asked Raymond for more information. Raymond testified that a couple of years earlier his then-four-year-old son had been pulling the family puppy's ears. Raymond and his wife both asked the boy repeatedly to stop it, but when the boy did it again Raymond pulled him away and delivered one short, swift swat with his hand to the boy's rear end. The boy had burst out crying and run to his room. Raymond felt terrible, but his wife told him he had done the right thing. The boy never mistreated the puppy again. Raymond never spanked any of his children again, and never would. He still felt terrible about it.

That courtroom scene is an example of how things can go right when a client and lawyer prepare for testimony. Raymond knew what the procedures were going to be like in the courtroom, and he could anticipate what kind of questions he might be asked. He knew he might be confused or uncertain, and he was prepared to pause, which allowed his lawyer to get the opposing lawyer to rephrase the question. I've seen it so many times, usually on the other side: An unprepared client might have testified no, I've never hit the kids. And then the opposing lawyer would bring up the spanking, and the client would not only look like a child beater but be exposed as a liar.

WHAT YOU SAY AND HOW YOU SAY IT

Failing to prepare to give testimony or interviews can be one of the stupidest mistakes a man makes when facing divorce. Whether in court or not, whether under oath or not, the casual, offhand, throwaway answer to a question can sink the case. On the other hand, a reasoned, cogent response—especially to a hostile question—can be the tipping point that turns the case in the man's favor, especially in custody contests. I want to emphasize that this is not always or exclusively a failure on the client's part.

Far too many lawyers do far too little to prepare their clients for testimony and interviews. Your lawyer should prepare you for what we lawyers call a "testimonial event"—typically a deposition, a hearing for temporary orders, or the trial—as well as for any other type of interview with outside experts or consultants. If your lawyer just tells you when to show up for the testimony or interview without reviewing the procedures and issues with you well in advance, you need to insist on meeting to prepare for what may be the most important interview you will ever have.

We'll delve more deeply into interviewing with experts and consultants later in this chapter, but I'd like to concentrate first on testimony that clients must give under oath. A deposition may be the first and is usually the most common of these testimonial events. It is often longer than testimony in court, because it is less formal and in a more conversational style. At a deposition, which is typically held in the office of one of the lawyers involved, the opposing attorney asks the client questions to elicit more information from the opposing party or to "lock in" the opposing party's version of events for use later at trial—especially if the opposing party's story changes. This is different from courtroom testimony that is intended to be focused and concise as to the issues before the judge. Because a deposition can be an attempt at a "fishing expedition" by opposing counsel, this can be dangerous territory for the man giving the testimony.

Too many clients are lured into a false sense of informality and talk too much during depositions. Our advice: Don't go past the four corners of the questions. Volunteer nothing. Say as little as possible. Be a minimalist. The lawyer sitting across from you may be nodding and smiling and encouraging you to talk, but that lawyer is not your buddy. That lawyer is trying to loosen your lips, and then use those words against you later. Remember, the sole purpose of the deposition is for the other side to get a preview of your case so they can better prepare to fight it later in court. Just as Raymond had been advised to pause before answering pointed questions during cross-examination, we urge every client to pause before answering each question in a deposition. This does two things. One, it lets him think about his response and keeps him from saying something he shouldn't. Two, it gives his lawyer—yes, your lawyer is with you at the deposition—a chance to jump in and object if the question is inappropriate. Conversely, your deposition is usually not the time to "defend" yourself. That gives opposing counsel more information that he or she may not have thought to ask about. So don't be surprised if your lawyer asks you few, if any, questions in your deposition.

Beyond the testimony in a deposition, a man involved in a divorce should expect to testify in court at some point, even if only briefly, either at a hearing for temporary orders or at a trial. The testimony at the temporary hearing may be limited to simply confirming or correcting the status of finances and custody, though it can be longer if there are significant disputes as to family situations. Testimony at a trial will be more detailed and can take an hour or days, depending upon the issues to be resolved by the court. However, the majority of cases are settled before a trial, without extensive courtroom testimony.

Let's talk about testifying in court. We saw in the opening trial scene how our client, Raymond, paused to think and gather himself, and avoided the trap about hitting his kids. No doubt his answer—"yes"—disappointed the opposing attorney, who was hoping for a "no" answer so that he could bring up the spanking, fluster Raymond, and hurt Raymond's credibility in the eyes of the judge. When asked a yes-or-no question, Raymond simply answered "yes." He didn't try to give a long-winded explanation, which is a good way to irritate a judge and open more issues for opposing counsel to explore. He was patient, and waited for re-direct examination for our attorney to allow him to explain and expand on the one-time spanking.

Much of the advice and preparation we give our clients—takin' the client to the woodshed, one of our lawyers in Texas calls it—applies to all types of tes-

Don't avoid preparing to testify or be interviewed just because you're nervous or uncomfortable or don't want to think about it.

timony or interviews. We caution against thinking you can stroll in and sit down and chat. You don't want to be your normal self. You want to be a smarter, calmer, more focused version of yourself. Don't avoid preparing to testify or be interviewed just because you're nervous or uncomfortable or don't want to think about it. The other side is going to try to make you look bad, to make you look unin-volved or uninformed, to get you to lose your cool.

The issue of tone is important. If you appear first and appear to be coherent, informative, businesslike, and an all-around reasonable person, the judge is going to appreciate that. Judges don't want to waste time. Their job is to get through cases. Unfortunately, divorce can be an emotional experience, espe-cially under the high-intensity spotlight of a courtroom. Equally unfortunately, displays of emotion in a courtroom—especially crying—can slow things down. Emotion is not supposed to be part of the legal process. I know it's difficult, but try to think of the terms of the divorce as a business deal.

If you can be more businesslike—and in my experience this is easier for men than women—you may have a subtle advantage. Women tend to show more emotion. They break down and cry. It's understandable. They probably haven't been in that situation before, on the witness stand, talking publicly about the failure of their marriage. But judges have been in that situation before. They've seen the tears and they've been trained to ignore them. Their focus is not on the emotion or on how someone feels or how badly someone has been hurt. Their focus is on the law and how the law applies to the facts of the case. That's all they want from witnesses and lawyers: facts. Not assumptions or suppositions or opinions or conclusions about what a bad husband the man is. Like Sergeant Joe Friday used to say on *Dragnet*, "Just the facts, ma'am."

HOW TO PREPARE

One of our lawyers once tried to prepare a client, a cowboy, for testifying at his divorce trial. He lived a couple of hours away and couldn't come in, but she got on the phone with him a few days beforehand and talked to him about the courtroom procedures and the types of questions he would be asked. She didn't give him specific questions—we don't do that because it can make the answers seem canned or rehearsed—but rather broader questions and topics that were sure to come up. She made sure he had all the documents in the case too. She asked him to read over everything and be prepared. But when he showed up for the trial and she asked him what he had done to prepare, he said, "I took a shower." He hadn't even looked at the material for the trial. On the stand, he was nervous, stumbled, answered questions he shouldn't have, and tried to give explanations at the wrong time. He did not have a happy result.

I want to emphasize, however, that all types of men fall into this trap. We have a surprising number of clients who are professionals and executives who have to be coaxed—or sometimes threatened, gently—to spend the time and effort on preparing for testimony and interviews. They think they are masters of their universe, able to cope with any lawyer or social worker or judge. There's nothing wrong with preparation and practice, we tell them. As one of our lawyers tells his clients, "You know why Phil Mickelson makes all those pressure putts? Because he practices . . ."

We can divide preparations into two categories: style and substance. Substance is always more important, of course, but let's talk a little about style—particularly how you look and act and talk. First, you want to look appropriate. You want to wear what's right for the occasion and for you. If you're a working-class guy and you're appearing in a court where the lawyers and judges are the only ones who wear ties, you'd look a little silly showing up in a three-piece suit. You're probably going to be nervous in the first place, and if you wear uncomfortable clothes you're probably going to be squirming and fidgeting and pulling at the collar and generally looking even more nervous and uncomfortable.

You don't want to wear work clothes or jeans, but maybe put on what you'd wear to a nice party or a job interview—slacks and a button-down shirt, maybe a sport coat. If you're an executive who usually wears a suit to work, wear the suit. But if you're pleading poverty in order to hold down your financial support to your soon-to-be-ex, don't dress flashy. A lawyer in another firm had prepared his client diligently for the questions at trial, and his client did well on both direct and cross examination. The client made some good points about being strapped for cash. Then, just as he was about to leave the stand, the judge learned over and said, "Excuse me, sir, is that a Rolex watch you're wearing?" The guy had to admit that it was, and his argument about not being able to afford child support went out the window. "I should have told him to leave the Rolex at home," the lawyer moaned later.

Think and talk about body language with your lawyer. The judge is going to be listening to the substance of the case, but also forming a general impression of you and what kind of person you are. You want to be calm and collected, as relaxed and "normal" as possible. Body language can be problematic for a man who is accused of being controlling or abusive, especially if he leans forward in the witness stand, speaks harshly, gets red in the face, or bangs his fists on the railing of the stand. Keep your face impassive. Don't sneer or roll your eyes, for example. One of the worst examples of body language our firm has seen came when the client—out of the blue—began leaning back and forth and swiveling around in the witness chair. He simply couldn't sit still. Our lawyer thought he was trying to look at ease and relaxed, but he kept bobbing and swiveling back and forth—at times his back was to the judge—so much that he came off as hyperactive.

The concern about body language doesn't end with your testimony. You will usually be seated with your attorney in front of the judge during the entire trial. Before and after your testimony, the judge may be observing your behavior at the counsel table as part of his or her assessment of you. Perhaps the best analogy is that you should conduct yourself at counsel table as you might in church—a polite interest in what is going on. Avoid visibly reacting to the testimony of other witnesses, or to the conduct of opposing counsel or the judge. Such reactions are often distracting to the judge or witness, and may give opposing counsel insight into a "hot button" he or she can attempt to use against you. We ask our clients to listen carefully during the proceedings and to take notes that we can review at the breaks.

When you speak, it may be difficult not to speak quickly or in an excited manner, but try to talk naturally and calmly. Don't use even a hint of sarcasm; it is seldom appreciated by the judge

and does not come across well in the transcript of the proceedings. Don't be flip. The opposing counsel may be sarcastic or give
a flip response in order to try to get you to respond in kind, but
don't do it. You don't want to look like a smart aleck.

Be careful with the words you use. You may get only one
chance to explain what you mean, so be as clear and concise as
possible. Jason was a client who came to us with a good chance
of getting joint custody. A social worker was assigned to his case
by the court, and Jason made a point of checking with his lawyer
every time he was about to meet with the social worker. In one
of these preparation sessions, Jason told our lawyer how he had
taken his five-year-old son with him to the grocery store that
week, and then they had taken their groceries back to Jason's new
house. The little boy was fascinated with the doorbell, and kept
ringing it. Jason asked him to stop and to come in the house.

"Just one more time?" the boy asked.

Okay, Jason told him, ring it one more time. The boy rang
it, and Jason held the door open for his son to come. Instead,
the boy stood there, stared at Jason, and rang the doorbell again.

"I stepped out," Jason said, "and gave him a kick on the butt,
he went into the house, and then . . ."

"Whoa, stop right there," our lawyer interrupted. "You kicked
him?"

"Nah, not really," Jason said. "It was more like a little tap,
a nudge, with my toe. That's just an expression—a kick in the
butt."

Our lawyer suggested that Jason use a different expression—
such as nudge—when talking with the social worker. He did,
and it was a good thing, because Jason's soon-to-be-ex later tried
to accuse him of child abuse for kicking the little boy. Because
Jason had used more-precise language to describe the incident,

the social worker already knew exactly what happened and didn't consider it abusive. The mom's complaint went nowhere.

This would be a good time to make a point about social workers. Too many men view the social worker as a sympathetic ear, someone who will listen as they pour out all the anger and frustration of their marital woes. That's a bad idea. The social worker is not your friend. The social worker is not your therapist. The social worker doesn't care about how badly your wife treated you. The social worker's only con-

cern is what kind of parent you are and what kind of parent you will be in the future. Keep your eye on that ball.

The social worker is not your friend or therapist.

Whether in court or not, under oath or not, you want to give the facts: the story of your relationship, your marriage, your family, and now your breakup. Don't be judgmental. Don't draw negative conclusions about her. Just give the facts. Don't try to use lawyer language, but do know what you are seeking in your case. Every state has different terms for different types of custody arrangements. Don't say anything you are not sure of. One of our lawyers once asked a woman on the stand, "What kind of custody arrangement are you seeking?"

"Permanent conservatorship," she said.

"Can you explain what that is, exactly," our lawyer asked her.

"Uh, it means I get the kids," she said. It doesn't mean exactly that, and she lost credibility in the courtroom for not even knowing what she was there for.

Think about the points you want to make. Why do you think you should have more time with your kids than your soon-to-be-ex wants you to have? Present the theory of your case. If your position is that she was a good stay-at-home mom, but now she's got to go to work and won't have as much time for the kids, while you're cutting back on work and hobbies in order to spend more time with the kids, stick to that position. Mention it over and over, in different ways. If she has started staying out late at night and leaving the kids with a babysitter, hammer away at that; mention it a dozen times. Too many men want to tell everybody about everything their soon-to-be-exes have done wrong, or what they think is wrong. Keep it simple and on point to the issues in your case. If there are three reasons you should get more time with the kids, mention those three things. If you are testifying about specific events in support of your position and are having trouble remembering all the incidents, say so: "I know there's something else, but I'm a little nervous and I've forgotten." If an opposing lawyer or anyone else ever asks, "Is that all? Are there any other examples of your wife's parenting that make you think you should have more custody?" then don't say no, there are no more examples. Say, "I know there are some others, but I just can't think of all of them right now."

Instead of being negative about their wives, men should be positive about themselves as fathers. They can elaborate on what they are doing to spend more time with their kids, and to make

Instead of being negative about their wives, men should be positive about themselves as fathers.

it more enjoyable and enriching for everyone. The dad wants to give examples of things he is doing that show he is a good father, and demonstrate

how much he loves his kids and wants to be with them. If a man can let that genuine love of his children come through in testimony or interviews, he is taking a giant step toward spending more time with them.

* * *

MUCH OF THE focus so far has been on testimonial events—depositions, hearings, and trials. Let's back up a bit and talk about experts and consultants who may play an important role, but whose interviews, conversations, and examinations may not be under oath. These consultants and experts include social workers, child service investigators, psychiatrists, psychologists, doctors, therapists, accountants, appraisers, and vocational or employment advisors. They may be appointed by the judge, but they are sometimes hired by one side or the other.

For example, it is not unusual for our client to hire a vocational or employment expert if the wife has not been gainfully employed during the marriage and wants maintenance (alimony) so she can continue to stay at home or to pay for her to obtain job skills. For the purposes of determining financial support, the court needs to gauge how much, if any, money she is going to need in maintenance payments from our client, her ex-husband. A big part of that equation is what she can earn on her own or what job skills she can reasonably obtain. Most courts expect ex-wives to get jobs, even if they haven't had one for a long time or have never had one. But what job? What is she qualified to do? How much can or should she earn? The soon-to-be-ex-wife's lawyers are going to assert that she has few marketable skills, and even if she can get a job she won't earn very much, or that she needs to obtain additional education—and the husband should pay more in maintenance.

We need our client to take the expert seriously and provide as much information as possible about his soon-to-be-ex—including information that would make her look good on the job market. It may be difficult for our client to "give the devil her due" and say she is organized, intelligent, outgoing, and motivated—traits that can help her in the job market. Our client also has to make the effort to go back over all the information he has ever known or learned about his wife's employments, or volunteering; he wants to show she has the ability to support herself.

You must be willing to open the books to your expert and not hold back or overstate matters. If there are concerns about sharing confidential business information, your lawyer can review whether it will be protected. If there are problems with the records being incomplete or inaccurate, your attorney and the expert can determine how best to proceed. Our clients who are self-employed or co-owners in family businesses often have financial records that may not be in the format used by accountants or auditors, creating the need for detailed discussions with our expert to explain the records. There may be errors in calculating depreciation, writing off bad debts, or tracking inventory. Again, these are issues opposing counsel is likely to uncover, so fully disclose everything to give your expert and attorney time to address any problems.

We insist on this type of preparation for all our clients, and for all their meetings with outside experts and consultants. Men facing divorce need to take all the experts and consultants seriously. Men need to prepare for these meetings, just as they would prepare for testifying at a deposition or in court. Indeed, sometimes their interviews with court-appointed experts are testimonial—the men's answers are on the record and may be cited by the expert later in court.

If an expert, investigator, or consultant calls you and wants to talk on the phone or set up an interview, put them off—politely, firmly, and vaguely. "I'm sorry, I can't talk right now. I'll have to check my schedule. Can I please call you back?" Then get on the phone with your lawyer. Talk about what you need to do to prepare. Your lawyer can and should describe the role of the expert, the procedure and rules of the interview, your goals, and what message you want to impart. If the interview is with an investigator, such as with a state child welfare office, your lawyer may wish to be present to observe and, if necessary, represent you. If the interview is with your wife's expert or consultant, our lawyers will often call the other side's lawyers and ask for the details of the meeting. If it's with a psychologist, are tests going to be administered? Exactly what tests? We'll send our client information on the tests, and maybe send him or direct him to some sample tests online so he can become familiar with them.

This is important, because a client's performance on a personality test is a fact, a statistic. It's something that a lawyer can point to and say, "This statistic indicates that this man is a control freak." That will mean a lot more to a judge than a disgruntled wife's testimony that her husband is a control freak. If she has some facts to back her up, it's a lot easier for the judge to believe her. If you are going to take a test, look it up and answer some sample questions. When you take the test for real, don't try to give the "right" answers. Most of these tests are designed to show when a person is being deceitful or dishonest. Answer honestly, but when you have a choice between (a) and (b), stay away from the one that might make you look worse. We once had a client try so hard to give the right answers that the psychologist called our lawyer and suggested that the client take the test over again. That was a break for us; if the psychologist had simply forwarded the results to the court with a notation that the client was being dishonest, it could have really hurt our case.

On the other hand, I once had a case in which the court ordered my client to seek counseling from a psychologist for anger management. The client knew he had an anger problem and was eager to get joint custody of his kids, so he went. I was pleased because he was doing the right thing. But after a couple of sessions with the therapist, my client decided this was the wrong therapist. He liked the anger management counseling but wanted to go to someone else who had been recommended to him. He switched therapists without consulting with me. When we were about to go to trial, I was surprised to learn of the change in therapists. It didn't matter to the judge that he had another therapist. The judge heard the other side talk about my client's anger, how our client had changed therapists when he decided he didn't like the first therapist, and that our client's therapy with the new therapist had not progressed to the point that the concerns for the children's safety were addressed. The judge awarded full custody to the mom.

Perhaps the most important court appointment in any custody case is the guardian *ad litem*. The GAL is typically a lawyer selected by the judge to represent the children in a custody contest. The theory is that Dad is represented by his lawyer and Mom is represented by her lawyer, each lawyer fighting for their clients; why shouldn't the kids be represented, too, by a lawyer who is solely on their side, looking out for their interests? Sometimes one or both sides in a custody contest will also hire their own outside experts, often called a child custody evaluator, but in most cases the GAL appointed by the judge can adequately investigate the day-to-day childhood issues such as schooling, home environments, and family interactions.

The GAL is independent—the two sides in the divorce case may be sharing the cost of hiring the GAL, but the GAL is not hired by either side or represent either side. The GAL might be appointed by the judge from a rotating list; your GAL may be whoever is at the top of the list when your case comes up.

Alternatively, the judge may first allow the attorneys to try to agree on a GAL. But in some courts judges can pick the GALs themselves, and they often pick them from lawyers they know and trust. It might be a former law school classmate, it might be someone the judge practiced law with, or it might be a lawyer the judge has seen in action in court many times. No matter how the GAL is chosen, however, it is important for men to remember that the GAL can have a huge influence on custody. The GAL gathers information from Mom, Dad, and often the kids themselves. Much of this fact-finding comes through interviews, particularly with the mom and dad fighting over custody. The GAL may also talk to other friends, relatives, neighbors, teachers, doctors, nurses, coaches, tutors, babysitters, and anyone else who might be around the kids or involved with them. The GAL then makes a recommendation to the court for when and where the children should be with their dad and mom, respectively. These recommendations are not binding on the court. Your lawyer usually will have an opportunity to examine the GAL in court as to the reasons for the recommendation and the information considered or not considered by the GAL. The judge doesn't have to follow them. But in the experience of the dozens of lawyers in our firm, judges do indeed follow all or most of a GAL's recommendations in the vast majority of cases.

Despite all that, too many clients—and their lawyers—don't take the GAL as seriously as they should. We see this from the moment the judge appoints the GAL. Our lawyers reach out to the GAL as soon as possible, sometimes on the courthouse steps right after the appointment. We want to make an appointment for the GAL's interview with our client. We do this right away for two important reasons: First, we want the GAL to see our client as responsible and credible, as someone who is on the ball;

second, we want our client to get his side of the story in front of the GAL first. It's just like the reason for filing for divorce first; when you get to tell your side of the story first, you're on offense and the GAL can pursue the issues with your wife from the start—putting her on the defensive. Telling your story first carries some weight.

One of the biggest mistakes we've seen clients make is not to follow up with a GAL. We'll talk to the GAL, who will say, "Great, I'd like to meet your client right away. Have him call my

One of the biggest mistakes we see clients make is not to follow up with the GAL.

office and make an appointment." We pass the contact information along to the client, who then does nothing. He doesn't call, he doesn't make an appointment. His soon-to-be-ex does call the GAL, however, and she makes an appointment, goes in, and gives her side first, putting our client on the defensive in that first meeting with the GAL. We not only lose the advantage of telling our story first, but we also look irresponsible to the GAL.

Once our client has an appointment—when you make that appointment, tell your lawyer right away—we sit down with him and prepare for the meeting with the GAL. Much of this preparation is similar to what we do for depositions, hearings, and trials, but with a few subtle differences. Unlike a deposition or a cross-examination, the interview with the GAL is not adversarial. The GAL may well ask challenging and provocative questions, or play the devil's advocate, but the GAL is not supposed to be on the mom's side. So it's particularly important for the dad who wants more custody, not less, to present himself as a good father: knowledgeable, competent, and cool under pressure.

Your lawyer might be with you at the interview with the GAL, or might not. We like to be there with our clients, local rules permitting, when the session with the GAL is a testimonial event—on the record. That's especially true if there are any hints of violence or criminal behavior in the case. We don't want our clients to incriminate themselves with a slip of the tongue or by misunderstanding legal technicalities. But sometimes our clients will meet on their own with the GAL, particularly if it seems like the GAL would prefer a one-on-one—and if our client is adequately prepared. Unlike many lawyers who spend little or no time preparing their clients for GAL interviews, we might spend an hour or more with a client going over documents, facts, and the framework of our case—just as we would for a deposition. Indeed, much of the preparation for a deposition carries over to a GAL interview, or vice versa, depending on which one occurs first in the case.

Whether or not his lawyer appears with him, it is up to the client to present his perspective in the most persuasive manner—based on facts, not on opinion or emotion. The GAL typically comes into a case knowing he or she is going to hear two very different versions of the facts, and that the truth is probably somewhere in between. Too many men wrongly seize upon the session with the GAL as yet another opportunity to trash their soon-to-be-exes, and that is unproductive and possibly damaging to the case. More than once, we've had clients spend the whole time with the GAL ranting against their wives. They know they're making a bad impression, but they can't help themselves. "Oh well," they say later. "At least I'll get a chance to tell my side of the story to the judge in court. The judge will believe my side of the story."

Men who think that are fooling themselves. As with social workers, conversations with GALs are an opportunity for men to show that they are good parents, that they will continue to be good parents, and that they deserve to have custody of their children. The time with the GAL might be their best opportunity in the entire process to get what they want in terms of custody. And if they blow it, they've probably blown it forever. It is unusual for a judge to reject a GAL's negative recommendation against a dad. If we think a GAL is going to be tough on our client, we suggest that we push harder for settlement rather than letting it get to the judge to decide custody.

The dad who wants custody needs to know the same things about his kids in talking to a GAL as he does when talking to an opposing lawyer at a deposition: schedules, friends, favorite classes in school, and so on. The dad needs to follow the same advice in terms of demeanor and language, and to remember what's important both in the overall approach to the case and in the minor details. Too many dads seem to think that every black mark against the mom carries the same weight. We've seen a client make a huge deal about his daughter coming home from her mom's with a splinter in her finger, and all but ignore the fact that his soon-to-be-ex was looped on painkillers the whole weekend she had the daughter.

Just as in depositions or court appearances, the dad has to know his goals and the facts of his case. The GAL is going to ask, maybe in different ways at different times, "What is in the best interests of your children?" And the dad has to have good answers. One of the best ways to get off on the right foot with a GAL is to speak reasonably, perhaps charitably, and maybe even a little sympathetically, about your soon-to-be-ex. At least at first. Then turn the conversation to the points you want to make: "My ex is a great person in many ways. She's always been a really gregarious person, very generous, very involved in community service. She's done many extraordinarily kind things for many people. It's just too bad she's let her good works and community service get in the way of our family life together."

Or: "My wife always worked hard and was a really diligent employee for her company. She was always the one her boss could call on to go the extra mile. But it seems like she put her work and her career—and eventually her friends from work—ahead of our marriage, and now that I'm not around to cover for her as much, it seems like her work is getting in the way of her taking care of the kids. I'm worried about her, and about the kids."

Or: "We were happy for a long time, but then gradually things began to change. We grew apart. I'm not sure why. But I'm sure it was as much my fault as hers. I think we both changed. I can't blame her for that. But I'm worried about how the changes she's made might affect her ability to take care of the kids. I've always been more of a homebody, and in recent years she's wanted more fun and excitement in her life. She goes out a lot more than I do, and in a way I envy her that. But it seems like if she's going to exercise classes and to the gym and out on a lot of dates, the kids are spending a lot of time with babysitters or with her relatives. I'm staying at home, and I'd rather the kids spend that time with me if they're not going to be with her."

One of the questions a GAL is likely to ask any dad in a custody contest is, "So, what do you think your wife is going to say about you?"

Some men who are unprepared or not in control of their emotions might say that anything she says about him is not true, and that the woman is a miserable liar. Other guys who are prepared will see this question for what it is—a golden opportunity to score points. It's an open-ended question that allows them, if they answer it carefully, to get their problems out in the open and talk about how they are dealing with those problems:

"My wife is going to say I'm an alcoholic. And she's right. I realize now that my drinking cost me my marriage. But I don't want it to cost me my kids too. Ever since we split up I've been going to AA. I haven't had a drop to drink, and I hope I never do again. I'm going to stick with it, because I love my kids and I want to be part of their lives."

Or: "Well, I hope she talks about all the good times we had together. We were so young when we got together, and we were so happy for a long time. I hope she'll talk about how we began to change and drift apart, and how difficult it was for me to accept that we were losing the love we had together. I hope she'll say I turned out not to be the right husband for her for the long run, but that I'm a good father."

Or: "She's going to tell you I am a violent person. I can see why she might tell you that, I guess. I used to get very angry with her, especially when she'd taunt me by flirting with other guys right in front of me, and then later when she began having affairs and didn't even try to hide it from me. I would get angry with her. I yelled at her. I said a lot of things I shouldn't have said, and wish I hadn't said. I can see how she might have thought those were threats. I'd just get so upset. Yeah, I threw things a couple of times, but not at her. I punched the wall a couple of times, but I never hit her. I haven't been in a fight since second grade, and I got my butt whipped then. I never hit the kids. I never will. One of the good things that's coming out of this divorce is that I've been going to a therapist who is helping me work through this anger, and showing me how to be more emotionally intelligent even if I get upset. I know when the kids get to be teenagers they'll probably do stuff that makes me crazy, but I know better how to deal with that now, and how to talk about it instead of yelling."

Take responsibility. Take ownership of your shortcomings. Take the high road. Don't talk about why she is a bad person. Talk about why you are a good parent. Embrace a measured, mature tone in the discussion, without being hostile or vindictive. But get your points

Take responsibility. Take ownership of your shortcomings. Take the high road. Don't talk about why she is a bad person. Talk about why you are a good parent.

across. The reason you want the kids is not that she's having sex with another man. The reason you want the kids is that you're a good parent and you love them and you want to be with them.

Tell the GAL your story. Talk about the history of the case, the history of your marriage, the history of the family, why you're in divorce court, and what your expectations are. Talk about your problems and your concerns. If you want more custody than your soon-to-be-ex wants you to have and she is asking for more child support than you can pay, speak frankly with the GAL about how if you had more time with the kids you wouldn't need to work as long and hard to meet their payments. Outline your plans, for yourself and for the kids, short term and long range. If you're going to be going back to school to get a master's degree, tell how the kids can stay with your parents while you're in class on Tuesday evenings.

Once in a while we'll get a client who not only fails to take a GAL seriously but behaves in a manner that is sure to make the GAL turn against him. Perhaps the most common example is when the dad goes off on a rant against the mom, and the GAL begins thinking, "This guy has so much hatred for his wife that he's going to alienate the kids from her." Another example is when a GAL helps arrange for a dad to have more temporary custody during the divorce proceedings—and then the dad doesn't use all that time. If a dad isn't using the time with his kids that he's being offered on a temporary basis, why should the court make it permanent?

We had one client who came out of his marriage determined to reinvent himself as the next Hugh Hefner. He wanted to be a playboy. He joined a website that arranged hookups between singles and invited people to post photos of their adventures having sex in public places. He put up a couple of photos of himself with a couple of different women in various stages of nudity in a park near his house. We tried to prepare our client for his interview with the GAL. We urged him not to boast about his new lifestyle or his exploits, but he did. He thought the GAL would be impressed with how well he was coping with divorce, and how well he was adjusting to single life. The GAL was not impressed, and especially was not impressed with the photos on the Internet. The GAL called our attorney and said, "Hey, this seems like a good guy who's going a little crazy right now. I'd like to look favorably on joint custody, but I can't do it if he is posting pornography."

We passed the word along to our client, expecting him to be contrite and to take down the offending photos. He wasn't and he didn't. "This is my lifestyle now," he told our attorney. "This is who I am." He was convinced that the GAL was a prude, and that the judge would see his philandering and frolicking as harmless adult fun. I am convinced that he would have gotten a good custody arrangement if he had followed our advice during preparations and followed the GAL's suggestions. I hope that wherever that guy is today, he is enjoying his life, because he's living it without his kids.

Remember how I wrote that the guardian *ad litem* is not on either side? Well, a dad who prepares and presents his case well can win over a GAL, and when that happens the GAL may well become an advocate for the dad in the courtroom, joining the dad's attorney in trying to persuade the judge to decide in the dad's favor.

Once in a while, whether from the luck of the draw or the judge appointing any attorney standing in the courtroom at the time, we'll get a "bad" GAL who does a shoddy job of interviewing, gathering the facts, and representing the children. One of my

> *A dad who prepares and presents his case well can win over a GAL, and when that happens the GAL may well become an advocate for the dad in the courtroom.*

colleagues had a recent case in Texas like that. Our client, Greg, was an accountant who wanted joint custody of his six-year-old son. His wife, who owned a bookstore, wanted to limit Greg's time with the boy to a few hours every other weekend. She didn't want him to have the boy overnight, ever. In that jurisdiction, a GAL typically files a report of around 40 pages, jammed full of interviews, school records, doctor's reports, and so on. In this case, the GAL filed a report of barely two pages. The GAL's recommendation gave the mom everything she wanted in terms of custody. Greg would get only five hours every second Saturday afternoon. That was it. The GAL's reasoning, as near as we could tell from the recommendations to the court, was, "The mom should have custody because she's the mom."

Greg was heartbroken. "What can we do?" he asked the lawyer in our firm representing him. We were able to put the case on hold until we could bring in our own child-custody evaluator, a psychologist who was trained in social work and specialized in family relations. Greg wasn't happy about the extra expense of hiring the outside expert, but he put everything into helping with that new report. He showed the new outside evaluator the room he had set up for his son in his new apartment. He lined up teachers from the boy's school to talk about how he was involved with his son's education. He arranged for a couple of mothers of his son's friends to talk to the evaluator about how he brought his son to playdates and often hung around to talk with the mothers about the kids and what was going on in their lives. Greg even had his son's Sunday school teacher talk to the evaluator about how Greg had always brought the little boy to class, but she hadn't seen the boy since Greg had moved out of the house.

Greg did everything he could to convince the evaluator that he was a good dad. "I know I'm not a perfect parent," Greg told her, "but I'm trying to learn to be better." He signed up for a class for divorced dads at the local YMCA, and began seeing a therapist who could help him work through his issues with his wife without projecting his anger at her onto their son.

The soon-to-be-ex, in contrast, figured she had already won full custody because of the original GAL's recommendation. She refused even to meet with our expert. That turned out to be a stupid mistake on her part. When the judge went through the two reports—the brief, cursory one from the GAL and the detailed, fact-laden, 55-page report from our expert—it was no contest. Our expert's recommendations were far more persuasive, and the judge made one of those rare decisions that went against the GAL's recommendations. Greg ended up getting what he asked for: joint custody.

DON'T MAKE A STUPID MISTAKE: PREPARE FOR YOUR TESTIMONY AND INTERVIEWS.

F YOU TALK to a man on his deathbed, and you ask him to name the most significant moments in his life, you're probably going to find out whether he ever went through a divorce. If so, he's almost sure to mention it. Almost every man who has ever been through a divorce remembers it as one of the most pivotal moments in his life. For many men, it is the single most important event in their lives—especially if it led them to become a better person, to forge better relationships with their children, or to find another partner who helped them find happiness and fulfillment.

The results of your divorce proceeding will be a huge factor in determining how the rest of your life goes: relationships with others, especially your children; finances; attitude; confidence; personality; and more. That's why it is so important for men facing divorce to arm themselves with the knowledge and fortitude necessary to make it through the divorce. The goal is not to win the divorce. Neither is the goal to merely survive it. The goal is to learn and grow.

You know how some men who have emerged from life-threatening illness and injury say it changed their lives and made them better people? How it has taught them to cherish their relationships and live each day to the fullest? Divorce, with all its angst and trauma, can provide the same sort of life-changing experience.

The key for most men is to gather the right information, but no one can do that alone—or with the help of one book and one set of guidelines, no matter how useful. We all need the right support team, starting with the right lawyer to help develop strategy and carry out tactics. Your "divorce support team"—friends, family, and especially your lawyer and all the resources of his or her firm—needs to function smoothly in order to be as efficient and productive as possible. It is an emotional time—perhaps the most emotional time of your life—and you need to feel like the team is supporting you and taking care of your needs and concerns.

Many men emerge from divorce with a new appreciation for those who support them. They learn, often for the first time, to seek out and nurture friendships. They have thrown themselves into knowing everything they can about the divorce process, and into the discipline required to help their lawyers develop a compelling case. Those commitments often help them embrace learning new things in other areas of life, and help bring self-discipline to their lives and devotion to the things that really matter in their lives.

By doing the right things and avoiding the stupid mistakes, men can remove the danger. That leaves the opportunity.

Yes, divorce is a crisis for most men going through it. But think of it like this: The Chinese symbol for crisis is actually a combination of two other symbols—danger and opportunity. By doing the right things and avoiding the stupid mistakes, men can remove the danger. That leaves the opportunity.

And that's up to you. If you have gotten this far in this book, you know that even in the darkest tunnels of divorce, there is a light at the end. You can step into it one day, feeling relieved and free and competent and confident as never before. Good luck.

INDEX

absentee fathers, 12
admissible evidence, 174–175
affairs and adultery, 61, 102–103, 176
after-dinner conversation, 151–152
alcoholism, 173–174
alienation, 114–115
anger management, 209–210
appraisals, 142
arguing, futility of, 158
arithmetic, credibility of accurate, 145
assets 87, 141–142, 143–144
associate attorneys, 43–44
attorney-client privilege, 84, 164–165
attorneys. *See* lawyers

balance sheets, 135
banking guidelines, 134
billing, 42–43
body language in court, 203
brick wall metaphor, 115, 120
business expenses, 136

case management systems, 48
checking accounts, 134
children
    alienation of, 13
    arguing in front of, 158
    case study, 105–107
    emotional fragility of, 114
    guardian *ad litem*, 81, 210–215

joint custody (*See* custody contests)
    moving out to protect, 11
    opinions and preferences, 114
    protecting the ex, 79–80
    on social networking sites, 176
clothing expenses, 139
clothing in court, 202–203
communication
    arguing, 158
    attorney-client privilege, 164–165
    case study, 148–151, 154–155, 156
    destructive, 157
    with friends and relatives, 158–159
    importance of, 35
    improper recording of, 159–161
    legal strategy, 165
    safe listeners, 153, 154
    using e-mail, 163
    with your lawyer, 45–47, 49–51
concealing information
    case study, 80–83, 93–94
    cheating wives, 102–103
    denial, 85–86
    domestic violence, 97–98
    drinking, 92–93
    extreme examples, 86, 90
    hidden assets, 87
    high-flyers, 86
    mental illness, 91–92

concealing information *(cont.)*
  parental irresponsibility, 98–100, 101–102
  perjury, 89–90
  post-divorce repercussions, 87–88
  pregnancy, 95–96
  skeletons in the closet, 103–104
conflict, avoiding, 11
Cordell & Cordell, P.C., 4–5, 39
court intervention, 11
credibility, 85, 129, 131
credit card statements, 161–162
credit cards, 134
credit checks, 134
crisis, Chinese symbol for, 222
custody contests
  alienation, 114–115
  changing parental roles, 113–114
  children's preferences, 114
  common sense, 110
  concealing evidence, 80–83
  cultural disadvantages, 108
  and Facebook, 173
  filing first, 71–72
  guardian *ad litem* testimony, 81, 210–215
  mental illness, 91–92
  and moving out, 12, 13
  objective evidence, 121
  parental role reversal, 116
  as punishment, 111
  stereotypes and double standards, 106–107
  substantiating involvement, 118–119
  and temporary orders, 14–16, 24–27, 186–187, 188–189
  too much communication, 148–151

denial, 85–86
depositions, 198, 199
destructive conversation, 157
discovery process, 184–185
disposable income, 136
disturbing the peace, 21–22
divorce
  economic considerations, 74–75
  emotional response to, 29
  lawyer's role, 131–132, 179–181, 198
  pivotal life moment, 221
  religious opposition to, 78
  as team effort, 186, 222
  as war, 56, 185
divorce law practitioners, 38–39, 46–47
divorce proceedings
  finalizing of, 12–13
  process, 50–51
  timelines, 12–13
domestic violence, 97–98
double standards, 116–117, 121–122
dumping the kids, 122

economic considerations, 74–76
electronic discovery, 174–175
electronic records, 162
e-mail records, 161–163
emergency protective orders, 11
emotion
  in courtroom testimony, 200–201
  stepping back from, 152–153
employment experts, 207–208
engagement, importance of
  case study, 179–180, 188–189, 191–192
  discovery process, 184–185
  "off the grid" clients, 181–183

quick trial dates, 190–191
temporary orders, 186–187,
188, 191–192
evidence, admissible, 174–175
expenses, 136
experts and consultants, 207–209

Facebook, 171–173
fairness, goal *vs.* reality, 107
false accusations, 11
family home, maintenance or sale,
17–18
family law
leeway in, 72–73
practitioners, 38–39
fees, 35–36, 40–42
Fifth Amendment, 84
filing first
at-fault considerations, 79
business valuation, 76
case study, 57–59, 63–64,
67–68, 68–69
communication and, 163
custody issues, 71–72
economic considerations, 74–75
financial settlements, 76
to freeze the situation, 57
health conditions, 62
husband's misconduct, 67–68
offense *vs.* defense, 64–70
potential for abuse, 59, 60
to secure better terms, 55–56
temporary orders, 14–16, 70–
71, 186–188
theory *vs.* practice, 57
venue, 62–64
financial and personal documents,
19–20
financial consultants, 208–209
financial records
balance sheets, 135

case study, 125–128
credit checks, 134
desired level of detail, 132–133
estimates *vs.* accuracy, 130–131
future income and expenses,
139–141
importance of, 128–129
income and expenditures, 135
credit cards and checking
accounts, 134
investment accounts, 135
lawyer's role, 131–132
reasonableness of, 146
financial settlements, 76, 137
finding a lawyer
advertising, 37–38
communication, 45–47, 49–51
divorce specialists, 38–39
gut decision, 32
initial consultations, 40, 45
lawyer referrals, 37
personal referrals, 36–37
questions to ask, 31–36, 52–53
retainers and hourly rates,
35–36, 42–44
when to do it, 30–31
"fishing expeditions," 198
food expenses, 138
freelance income, 135–136
friends and relatives, 158–159
future financial requirements, 140
future income, 141

GAL (guardian *ad litem*), 81,
210–220
gambling losses, 177
going to trial, 12, 47–48, 48
GPS surveillance, 161–162
grandparents, 26–27, 189
guardian *ad litem* (GAL), 81,
210–220

harbor pilot metaphor, 50
health conditions, 61–62
hidden assets, 87
high-flyers, 86
hostile divorce, 17–18
hourly rates, 41–44
household inventory, 19–20
household maintenance and repair, 139
hypochondria, 62

income and expenditures, 135, 137
infidelity, 61, 102–103, 176
initial consultations, 40, 45
in-laws, relationships with, 159
interrogatories, 184–185, 186
interviews. *See* testimony and interviews
investment accounts, 135

joint accounts, 161–162
joint assets, 141
joint custody. *See* custody contests
judge's role, 12–13
judicial bias, 108, 112
judicial discretion, 72–74

keeping secrets, 168
key logger software, 161, 169
kidnapping charges, 72, 106

lawyers
    mistakes made by, 192–193
    replacing, 193–194
lawyer's role
    decision to divorce, 77–78
    financial records, 131–132
    testimony and interviews, 198, 209–210
Leave It to Beaver households, 109
legal fees, 40–41

legal separation, 78–79
legal strategy, 165
lost documents, 60

miscommunication, 164
mistakes, common tendency to make, 1–2
moonlighting income, 135–136
moving out
    alternatives to, 12
    author's advice, 10
    case study, 9–11, 27–28
    custody contests, 24–27
    do-overs, 11
    financial considerations, 16–17
    good reasons for, 9
    household inventory, 19–20
    household maintenance, 18
    and joint custody, 13–14
    legal argument, 17
    moving back in, 21–25
    personal property, 20–21
    reasons to avoid, 12
Mr. Mom, 58

neglecting the children
    alienation, 114–115
    case study, 105–107

"off the grid" clients, 181–183
online activity, 166–178
    case study, 175, 177
    online personas, 170–171
open-ended promises, risks of, 152–153
out-of-court settlements, 12

paralegals, 43–44
parental irresponsibility, 98–100, 101–102
parenting, 112

perjury, 89–90, 142
personality tests, 209–210
phone records, 161–162
pleading the Fifth, 84
police involvement, 11
preparation and control, 30
private investigators, 61
promises, risk of making, 152–153

quick trial dates, 190–191

red flags, 21
referral fees, 37
researchers, 43–44
retainers, 42

safe listeners, 153, 154
Second Life, 177–178
secrets, 168
settlements, 48
skeletons in the closet, 103–104
social networking, 167–173
spousal mischief, 17–18

team approach, 131–132, 186
temporary orders, 14–16, 70–71,
    186–187, 188
testifying in court
    appropriate language for,
        204–205

body language, 203
case study, 204–205
guardian *ad litem,* 210–215
lawyer's role, 198
testimony and interviews, 198,
    199–200
case study, 194–197, 201, 218,
    219–220
displays of emotion, 200–201
experts and consultants,
    207–209
owning shortcomings, 214–217
style and substance, 202–203
trash talk, 152, 163

unfair assumptions, 3–4
user names and passwords,
    169–170

venues, 47
"virtual life," 169
virtual reality, 177–178
vocational experts, 207–208

war analogy, 56, 185
wiretapping, 159–162
women lawyers, 39–40